Ripening

AN AUTOBIOGRPHY

GERALD MIDDENTS

RIPENING
AN AUTOBIOGRPHY

iUniverse books may be ordered through booksellers or by contacting:

iUniverse
1663 Liberty Drive
Bloomington, IN 47403
www.iuniverse.com
844-349-9409

ISBN: 978-1-6632-3530-5 (sc)
ISBN: 978-1-6632-3531-2 (e)

Print information available on the last page.

iUniverse rev. date: 01/22/2022

CONTENTS

I. INTRODUCTION:

A. EARLY EXPLORING

We are all planted by our parents!
Whose hopes show in the firmament!
We grow like plants in their garden!
Feeding AND protection was inherent!

We are nurtured and also educated!
Our achievements made them elated!
Our foibles became learning experiences!
Taking risks to help us deal with chances!

Responsibilities help us to mature!
Physical and social human nature!
We are "green" while growing up!
Shaping our personalities to cope!

Ripening becomes inherent naturally!
Turning from green to grow maturely!
Joining with others for connections
Continuing to share joint expectations!

Ripening is a usual development;
When there is no interference.
But life is not always normal;
While sometimes it is unusual.

A few persons live beyond 100,
More women do this then men.
Some maintain their mentality,
Which helps them to be happy.

Predictors suggest more centurions.
Are more likely among Americans.
Retirement is up to sixty-seven.
Others predict earlier retirement.

B. ACADEMIC STUDIES

Schools were not difficult for me
My 8 years in school in the county.
In this school, I had one classmate!
One room in Liberty Number 9!

A small town, Kamrar High School
Only twelve classmates four years.
I played on teams of two sports;
Basketball and also Baseball!

One classmate later became my wife!
In High School years, we had one date!
Then in my last years at Iowa University
She was a Teacher as we went steady!

The Korean War was just happening
An Air Force cadet, I would be serving.
I graduated "With Highest Distinction!"
This achievement gave me momentum!

RE-BALANCING

As we ripen, there is need for balancing!
Responsibilities may call for "re-directing!"
To a calling for the rest of our own living!
Plus mentoring plus also volunteering!

We may offer helpful active sharing!
And also, by our reciprocal exchanging!
May lead to additional cultivating!
Positive times are also rewarding!

An analogy is re-balancing tires!
Even the best rubber tires will wear!
Car speed up but need to hold on curves!
Wheels can get out of wear taking swerves!

Even our shoes show wear on our own heels!
In contrast to living creatures who restore!
Healthy living with risks can then recover
Life span is extended by being healthier!

One-sidedness calls for re-balancing!
With femininity and masculinity maturing!
By shaping our personalities more fully
Socially, physically and also spiritually!

Exciting our brains more expansively!
Incorporating stimuli connectively!
Both locally and also globally!
So that we engage cosmically!

LIFE's CALLINGS

Discovering one's callings is helpful!
Investing energy in what is hopeful!
Matching one's talents in what is fruitful!
Contributing to others is being soulful!

Humanity benefits from many callings;
Both values and one's faith for serving!
Dedication motivates us to do our best!
We can then claim we earn our rest!

Doing one's calling grows into ripening!
Fruit and seeds we can then be bearing!
Becoming fruit will then be gratifying!
Assuring our efforts are continuing!

Leaving our heritage is purposeful!
Even combining joys and tears full!
Convinced one's existence is fruitful!
Hoping peoples' lives are plentiful!

BEQUESTING

Hopefully we have our legacy to give.
Beyond material goods to value our leave!
Posterity with value ideals as a heritage!
Plus, our offspring from a loving marriage!

These personal gifts are also intangible!
To assist future generations to be capable!
Thru fostering higher levels of civility!
Balancing all this with humility!

These experiences fill life with meaning![1]
Such fulfillments make life worth living!
Pack them with both ideals and action!
Emerging in expanded to its maximum!

---

[1] See author's book on <u>Personal Meaning DeMystified.</u>

Sharing with posterity is very essential!
Helping next generations reach potentials!
Having inherited the past was generous!
Passing forward gives them an inheritance.

B. SPROUTING SEEDLINGS

SPECIAL SEASONS FOR LIVING

This quartile of living presents us with challenges & opportunities,
In "The Seasons of Human Life," we re-launch with springtime.
Then our chronological sequences—summertime, fall and winter,
We human beings can pursue purpose and personal curiosities,

SPRINGTIME

In nature, life emerges in the spring with sprouts and activities,
New growth spurts forth out of the earth nesting proclivities.
Children get restless "to get out to do things" unconfined,
Kids, animals, plants and birds innately know spring has emerged.

School children waffle restlessly with energy to be outdoors,
Boys are eager to play ball, go fishing and swim on the shores.
Girls create their activities like biking to visit friends & families,
Traveling to camp, plus tease boys who smaller until mid-teens.

Colorful imaginations stimulate youth in expansive experiences,
Exploring, stretching their skills, widen readiness for adventures.
Mischief has both pros and cons that being troubles and successes,
Self-directed play creates special skills plus new creative processes.

Springtime in life lays solid foundations upon which to grow,
Planting seeds in this season with expectations about what to sow.
Protecting sprouts, watering and weeding, cultivating as humans,
Siblings help, siblings fight, sibling rivalry of young men and woman.

SUMMERTIME

After rapid spurts of growth, launching from the nest is attempted,
Slips and falls plus ups and downs are part of becoming developed.
Like eagles growing, flapping their wings, bodies are strengthened,
Minds and bodies, skills and falls all accumulate as days lengthened.

Nature's Summer Parades draw up to engage in outdoor activities,
Plants accelerate their beauty, flowers attract the birds and bees.
Water invites us to jump in for cool swimming; lakes for fishing,
Sailboats glide through challenging waves of ocean's breaking.

"Going to Camp" excites adventurous youth but not all introverts,
Friendship enriches, new skills grow as we become natural experts!
Traveling and camping involve us into adventures into the unknown,
Stories and photos refresh our favorite memories to be later shown.

FALL

Fall is a mixture of maturing harvests and also schools beginning!
Days become shorter while fall colors come out with full bursting!
New classes and classmates expand us to engage our curiosities,
Sports enlarge our physical coordination plus our dexterities.

In alternate year, campaigning for those seeking to serve in office,
Candidates attempt to chance as attractive stars trying to entice.
Agricultural communities become excited about their harvesting,
Numerous celebrations and holidays invite to engage in feasting!

Sports have full seasons for the World Series plus a football game,
Teams display their talents, battling contests and search for fame.
Season of Thanksgiving are festive while Holidays are proclaiming,
Families plan very special occasions for celebrating and sharing.

WINTER

Preparations anticipate long winter of hibernating and reclusions,
  Animals adapt their furs to be warmer, woollier than other seasons.
Storing up food for survival plus resting yearlong work and tensions,
  Festive celebrations, winterized dwellings plus holiday preparations.

Designated as year's end, winter is also for new expectant planning,
  Completing projects, paying taxes, plus advent season observing.
The seasonal cycles provide rhythm necessary for human renewing,
  Dormant seasons are actually very active for futures with hoping!

Seasons of Life re-introduces human search for personal meaning,
  Jointly planning for the future year provides us new beginnings.
Cycles build up our capacities for new starts for enriched living,
  Spiraling into the future ahead calls us for greater energizing.

HUMAN RIPENING

People respond with curiosity
  When they launch an inquiry:
    A friendly "How are you doing?"
      Here then is a way of replying:

        My response if "I'm ripening!"
      Quickly they respond by smiling.
    Now this may prompt repeating
  Smiles do the communicating!

Fortunately, I am feeling well;
  Into my late-80's: I can tell!
    White beard and white hair;
      This is a pleasant way to share!

Good vision helps me for seeing,
But I have very limited hearing.
I need to watch person's lips
Sometimes missing key clips.

Most people understand ripening;
By associating fruit for enjoying
The immature fruit tastes sour
Ripening does make it better!

Ripening occurs to be contented;
Rather than a time to contend.
Yes, there might be struggles
But living also has its troubles!

Both plants and fruits need seasons;
Humans comprehend the reasons.
Nature does facilitate growing
As maturity involves ripening!

Many people plant gardens;
The have learned to start one.
Yes, gardens take our energy
So, a harvest requires plenty!

They wait for them to late ripen
Beans, peas and lettuce turn green.
Cabbage grows "heads" and leaves,
Growers watch them to be pleased.

Some others ripen differently,
They mature very colorfully!
Squash turn a deep yellow;
As does corn to be mellow.

Beets become deep purple;
Radishes are read or yellow.
Watermelons are red inside,
While they are green outside!

Cherries ripen to redness
Likewise do strawberries.
Grapes become deep purple
Bright red glow like apples!

Cantaloupe turns deep orange;
While outside they are grey.
There are also white potatoes
Plus, bright orange potatoes!

Gardeners do know vegetables;
That makes them very capable!
Their own families are healthier
And they are also much stronger!

Ripening becomes a joyful time;
Cooks may add tasteful "thyme!"
Balanced diets are the big key
As people can eat with glee!

These fruits and vegetables
Develop seeds to reproduce!
They permit them for continuing
This also allows regenerating!

The good fruits and vegetables
Develop seeds for reproducing1
This permits their continuing
It also does allow regenerating!

So ripening is then essential;
Seeds lead to great potential!
These processes are in nature
For reaching to fuller stature.

Yes, nature is very amazing!
It does merit our appreciating.
We humans are key facets
Part of nature's real assets!

Whooops!!! I forgot parsley,
Maybe we need a Parsley Day!
Now, you may think about others
Vegetables have sisters and brothers!

A few that my Mother never served:
In our own family, no rutabaga!
We never-ever had arugula!
Nor do I recall any jicama!

I knew all about good carrots!
Later learned about coconuts.
Yes, we recommend grapefruit
But I have not had "jackfruit!"

Yes, there are many berries;
I learned to love raspberries!
Plus eating many blackberries;
Late to consume boysenberries!

My wife makes spaghetti squash!
Have you had butternut squash?
It got sick after eating rhubarb;
But, I love strawberry rhubarb!

Rhubarb needs real ripening;
If too green, it is sickening!
There is so much to learn;
And we must also earn.

C. RELATING TRUST & LONELINESS

Jointly, trust and loneliness interact!
   Many stages of living and contract!
      Both these factors can be significant!
         For most people these are Important!

         Becoming the center of attention
      Provides non-verbal comprehension!
   As the focus of parents' relationship
An infant feels much more significant!

Words do not fully carry this meaning!
   But nearness highlights infant's being!
      Such intimate contact is so valuable!
         Both parents and infant as personable!

         Trust can develop very early in living!
      Involves a child and parents connecting!
   Children learn from dependable parents!
Permitting both trusting in developments!

Trustworthy parents enrich growing up!
   Children trust adults as giving new a cup!
      Nourishment is so essential for growth!
         Plus, comforting care and being secure!

Growth from infancy to early childhood
   Exploring one's environment does help!
      Safe interactions with siblings and friends!
         Handling separation, anxiety develops!

         Playing with other children is creative!
      Hopefully favorable times are positive!
   Yes, tuffs and pouting occur readily!
Testing how a child learns security!

Enjoying playmates becomes essential!
Friendly trusting can foster potentials!
Activities and schools foster maturing!
Inherent growth comes with interacting!

Bringing friends home is helpful!
Children benefit by being trustful!
Yes, there are times of loneliness,
This cultivates more inventiveness!

TRIALS for TEENS

Chums inherently counter loneliness!
They fulfill each other needs & trust!
Many teenagers have times alone!
Often relying heavily on a phone!

But being alone can be essential
Self-confidence is mostly crucial!
Individuality emerges and blossoms!
Transpiring overcomes some gloom!

Teen years are typically very distinctive!
Balancing social and individual as unique!
Dating may occur somewhat naturally!
Pondering who may be trustworthy!

Chronically lonely youth feel solitary!
Healthy relationships they may envy!
"Being ready for invitations" can help!
Letting others know who will support!

Self-doubts may erratically come and go!
Fragile persons may have a volatile ego!
Re-assurance with support from others,
Who know about sisters and brothers!

Volatility in relationships is normal!
Teens learn to manage conventional!
Trusting vs. mistrusting aids maturing!
Resulting in experience for adult living!

EARLY ADULTHOOD

Adolescence is extended in society!
Factors include education and military!
In many cultures, teenagers mature!
Out of necessary so they can endure!

In advanced societies comes adulthood!
Challenging inexperienced young adults!
Yes, opportunities can become available!
Demanding that early adults are capable!

Seeking social relations is very natural!
Filling their times to what is available!
Drugs and alcohol can be a problem!
Jeopardizing maturity can happen!

When mating occurs, time is precious!
Partners find "give and take" a challenge!
Careers and parenthood can be fulfilling
As couples find challenges as thrilling!

Now opioids can provide highs artificially;
But addictive and also death possibly!
Current tragedies become notorious
Too late, dangers become obvious!

Research reveals thirties can be lonely!
Adult responsibilities need capabilities!
Cultivating relationship can be helpful!
Facing the tasks of being accountable!

MIDDLE YEARS

There are many reasons for stability
Aided by relationships with many!
Family, friends and other relations
May flourish on many occasions!

Widowhood may be formidable!
An initial loss provides many trials!
Loss of a trustworthy one happens
That presents even more challenges!

Fortunately, friends and family are helpful!
Plus, new relationships can be valuable!
Widows often can handle such a loss!
Different challenges for new widowers.

Being single again is an experience!
It may be a grave time of loneliness!
Helpfully, evidence provides support
New relationships take an effort!

People seemingly do live longer
By developing new set as trustful!
Supportive relations become helpful
When either younger or also older!

Research on relations support religion!
Providing fellowship and connection!
Spiritual development may continue
Providing secure anchors in religion!

Mutuality is practiced as spirituality!
Affirming each person individually!
Moreover, faith provides assurance
That undergirds further confidence!

Moreover, volunteering is helpful
Both to the receivers and givers!
Powerful relationships may occur
Supporting both parties to endure!

AFFIRMATIONS

Trustful relations may be affirming!
Enriching our lives in positive doing!
Engaging others is very supportive
Making friendships as effective!

Giving attention to others' needs!
Uplifts all parties to then succeed!
Religious avenues serve this role;
Providing mutuality as a goal!

Persons develop trustful relations!
Affirming such new participations!
Meaningful relations then build!
With importance and new thrills!

Loneliness can also be overcome!
For persons together to be chums!
Friendliness becomes also nurtured!
By engaging with persons as affirmed!

II. EXPANDING OUT

Over decades, cross-cultural experiences
Contribute to my personal enrichments!
These mostly happened beyond college
While providing valued experiences!

While I was serving in the Air Force
Stationed near Albuquerque, N. Mexico
Our Squadron had men from other cultures
Including Blacks and Mexican-Americans.

As Squadron Adjutant with many duties
I learned about soldiers from cultures.
Naturally, we had a number of Hispanics
Who sought this base for assignments.

These were very conscientious personnel
Very capable of being of being mechanics.
They handled aircraft very conscientiously
Proud to be serving in the nation's military.

I recall they were very respectful,
Displayed in their job performance.
They earned their military rank
They earned the pilot's thanks!

Mexican food became a treat;
I love enchiladas for a meal to eat.
Food becomes an expression of culture
So today are many Mexican restaurants.

I wish that I had learned to speak Spanish
We need to learn more than only English.
Multiple languages are now essential
Enriching most everyone's potential.

GROWING to MATURE

Northwestern Bell Telephone hired me
I became a management trainee.
The Air Force called me to duty
At Kirtland AFB, Albuquerque.

Assigned as Air Force Squadron Adjutant;
With only six officers and 250 Airmen.
This involved numerous duties;
Promoted to First Lieutenant.

Lt. Colonel Fulton as Commander,
With twenty-six Master Sergeants!
They ran this Air Force Squadron
So we did fulfill our mission.

Col Fulton arranged a flight
To have it stop at Des Moines.
This was Mothers' Day weekend
So Arlys and I became engaged!

A. LIKING NEW MEXICO

Why do we love the state of New Mexico?
There are many reasons for our support!
Scenery is an obvious is very obvious!

Arising with the sunrise as mysterious!
Variety describes reasons for loving
Many colors for everyone beholding!

Living in New Mexico in the Air Force,
Not in Korea for my military service!
Battling in Korea was much worse!

Working with Airmen and Scientists!
A Squadron and Base Ass't. Adjutant;
As our Base tested Nuclear Weapons!

As a young officer, experiences occurred
Being responsible for the official orders!
Protecting Nation's TOP SECRET Security!

Learning challenges of accountability!
Colleagues career officers and scientists!
Plus experience in management risks!

BECOMING MARRIED!

During service, my 1ˢᵗ marriage happened!
As High School Classmates, we were acquainted!
Arlys enjoyed New Mexico as our first home!

She taught in a private school with charm!
Other young couples were readily engaged!
Each Sunday, we sang in a Church Choir!

Enjoying Santa Fe become very intriguing!
Falling in love with the Indian paintings!
Visiting Pueblos proved to be exciting!

Plus, turquoise jewelry for purchasing!
Seasons were beautiful to experience
Hispanic foods were also delicious!

A repelling item were fierce dust storms!
Arizona's dust passing through to Texas!
The next day might become a reversal!

When dust returned going to Arizona!
But the weather was very moderate
Compared to the Midwestern climate!

Our families would come to visit us!
Adjusting to New Mexico without fuss!
My Mother did not like Mexican Food!

But this new territory was nicely cool!
The mountains were always visible!
Plus, Native American and Hispanics!

Became married, August 21, 1955.
Then assigned as Ass't. Base Adjutant.
Responsible for TOP SECRET Documents!
Plus approve the Base Daily Orders!

With a TOP SECRET Security Clearance
Even yet greater responsibilities!
Ten Airmen reported to me
Plus, two civilian Secretaries!

The Korean War was settled!
    My tour of duty was reduced.
        Back to NW Bell employment
            Offered a role in Management.

B. CALLED into MINISTRY

        Then I had a decision to make;
      About God's Call to ministry!
Then I enrolled in Seminary
Accepted a role at University.

Became Director of Men's Housing;
    With 210 students for supervising.
        My Air Force duties were fitting
            All in Main building for living.

        Then came another good option:
      Arlys could study for graduation!
She earned his Bachelor's Degree!
Then she did teaching when free.

        Men saw her as Dorm Mother!
      As she was my first Partner!
I supervised these college men;
Only very few were veterans.

My studies went very well;
    Third year was a challenge!
        Student Minister on weekends;
            Studies and sermons to prepare!

Arlys was now pregnant!
Thanksgiving, Susan arrived!
She was our special blessing
With parenthood for learning!

Graduated Masters of Divinity!
Honors: Magna cum Laude!
Had an excellent experience
Then Ordained as Minister!

Called to a Church near Minneapolis.
With wide range of responsibilities.
Served with the Senior Minister;
Responsibilities also to administer.

Special role with Senior Highs;
Also did survive with all ages!
Bought a house for our family
Wife and daughter all happy!

Learned to care for our property;
We had approximately 25 trees!
I painted the house's siding
Plus did regular lawn-mowing.

Church youth were also invited
Dozens of Senior Highs participated!
Our youth program gained attention;
Helped three other congregations.

Invitations came to speak at retreats;
We also performed with dramas.
We had very creative programs,
These were featured at conventions!

On January 10, 1963, Gregory was born!
As an infant, he was 9 and ½ pounds.
Nurse: "Strong enough to walk!"
-30 degrees F. coming home!

Winter in cold Minneapolis!
But we were used to this.
Snow banks to be scooped!
Winter clothing to be worn.

The Presbyterians encouraged studies
Awarded grant for doing a Ph.D.
Psychology was my preference;
For Teaching and for practice.

On Sundays at congregations
I moderated and gave sermons.
Helped two Churches re-unite;
Three others to invite new pastors.

One summer came another role;
To do research for new Church sites.
Promising locations were identified
Plus, two experiments to be tried.

My Doctoral advisor was helpful;
A leading authority on creativity,
Paul Torrance known internationally;
I was his Assistant for two years.

Served part-time in campus ministry
An experience was a "Bar Ministry!"
Engaged loner's personal needs
Minnesota U. expanding rapidly!

Asked to Coordinate Campus Ministries
But I preferred teaching on Faculties.
Accepted a role at Austin College, Texas.
Engaged in steps to change locations.

New role invited me to do planning;
Arlys came along to find housing!
This quickly led to do building
New house became exciting!

So we sold our house on Lake Street!
We packed up belongings complete!
We took Lake vacation for a week!
Visited relatives in Iowa for a week!

Authorship of Professional Publications:
A COMPARISON of PARENTAL and ADULT LEADERS in
PERCEPTIONS OF CHURCH YOUTH. M.A. degree at
University of Minnesota,1965.
THE RELATIONSHIP of CREATIVITY and ANXIETY, Ph.D.
Dissertation,
University of Minnesota, 1967.

C. TEXAS!

August 13, 1967, we arrived in Sherman!
Our eyes wide open for Westside Drive!
New house completed with new lawn!
Susan and Greg each had a bedroom!

We settled right for our new home!
Moved our furniture into each room.
This was very exciting for our family!
Plus started to settle at Austin College!

The Fall semester would start shortly
So, I arranged the syllabi quickly.
Two Counseling Services open
Needed to hire a Receptionist!

Margaret Crow was my Secretary
She had served at the Air Force Base.
Plus, an experienced Counselor for youth
Serving the High School Senior Highs.

Alice Parks served as their counselor
Her husband died so she was a widow.
She also was finishing her Masters
Serving youth for making life plans.

This Service for Presbyterian Youth
They came from four state-synod.
College students were my clients
Both personal and for careers!

Taught two courses at Austin College!
One was in "Personality Development."
A graduate course on "Counseling Theories;"
This was also composed of sharp students!

Yes, this was a very busy first semester!
Requests to conduct Worship Services.
The week and weekends were busy
New Colleagues were great to meet.

Colleagues became very supportive;
Our new house was also very livable!
The City of Sherman was delightful;
Plus, new neighbors were likeable!

My courses had graduate students!
Their performances were excellent!
Some did thesis research on creativity
They represented very wide diversity!

The counseling load was very heavy!
This occurred in the nineteen sixties!
One colleague provided some help;
Assistance from a graduate student.

I was able to hire this graduate
Charles Schroeder was very able!
I could retain him as a Counselor
He and wife, Barbara, were helpful!

We invited them to attend conventions;
In 1968, after ML King's assassination.
Both Alice and Charles came also
We had expansive experiences.

Alice a widow was also pursued
By a Physician from North Texas.
They asked me to do their wedding;
This became a special blessing!

The next year was in Las Vegas
APGA was helpful with cases.
I introduce Charles to G. Wrenn,
A Leader in Student Development!

Barbara was extremely excited!
TV Danny Thomas had stopped her
Telling Barbara his impression!
She reminded him of his daughter!

Charles went on to earn his Ph.D.
He became known nationally!
A leader in College Personnel
Became V-P at Universities!

Texas authorized Professional License
I was in the first group to be licensed.
This was an additional credential
When testifying in Court Trials.

We needed an additional Counselor;
Two Texas Universities nearby.
So I served as a Supervisor
Helping to gain Licensure.

Then I advised Dorothy LeMole
As a Ph.D. candidate at ETSU.
She was also very experienced
We were pleased how she served.

Next, I hired Harry Heiser;
He was an excellent Counselor!
The 1970's were demanding;
Students needed counseling!

Colleagues were very helpful;
The "70's" were "challenge-full!"
Both undergraduates and graduates
Created exciting academic "basketsful!"

The Head of the Biology Department
He and I created new compartments!
Medical Schools hoped for evaluations
To understand pre-medical students!

Psychological tools were helpful,
And to educate pre-meds as valuable.
Experience in assessing other professions
Provided data for medical education.

Medical School Officials suggested
That I publish the procedures used.
The Journal of Medical Education[2]
Published my brief recommendations.

Thirty-five inquiries were received!
These Medical Schools were pleased.
Professions benefit from Psychology
To educate their own student body!

I had previously published a report
That summarized my Dissertation.[3]
This research was on creativity
And anxiety in multi-correlation.

My publications of 1970's:
Journal of Religion and Health, Vol. 9 No.3 July 1970.
THE PSYCHOLOGY of ENEMY-MAKING and PEACE-MAKING,
1972.
"The Effect of Two-way Interactive Television on the Racial
Attitudes of Sixth Grade Students." 1973 (editor).
"Methods for Assessing Professional Qualities, JOURNAL of
MEDICAL EDUCATION, 1976. Over 35 inquiries from
Medical Schools.

---

[2] Middents, G., 1976, "Procedures for Assessing Pre-Medical Students," The Journal of Medical Education

[3] Middents, G., 1973, "The Relationship of Creativity and Anxiety," The Journal of Religion and Health.

With an inheritance from Mother Estate
I purchased the Sherman Steam Laundry.
This 10,500 sq.ft. building was empty
Plus, a nearby garage on 1 ¼ acres.

The owners were asking for $85,000
I offered $40,000 and they agreed.
So, Tom Nuckols and son, Tommie
Plus, Susan and Greg did painting.

Quickly, I had six renters for storage!
This 99 year old building restored!
Located two blocks from downtown
A family project that had renown.

In six years came a special offer:
$113,500 that I quickly accepted!
It was turned into an office building.
Plus "The Sherman Steam Laundry Café!"

I pursued Multi-Disciplinary studies.
Became Chair of Program on Policies!
I had been teaching Health Care Policy
Plus, courses that we Inter-disciplinary!

At Austin College, we taught in teams;
These were from various disciplines.
Yes, we were on the cutting edge;
Going beyond formal departments.

More Psychologists came to Texoma;
One special colleague was Bob Beck.
We started Texoma Psychological Assoc.
Members gained to about eight colleagues.

We arranged conferences for re-licensing!
These workshops were worth attending.
In 1987, I invited Dr. George Vaillant,
Psychiatrist at Harvard Medical School.

Our three-day Conference at Texoma;
Delegates from D-FW and Oklahoma.
This was a very successful event!
Psychologists found it worth it!

PROFESTIONAL PUBLICATIONS of 1980's:
THE GIFTS of LIFE: GIVING AND RECEIVING. 1988.

D. RAIN-DANCING and POETRY WRITING

When it is dry, people want rain;
When it is wet, they want poetry!
So, I am busy most of the year,
This helps me to bring cheer!

In the Southwest, people dance;
They want rain, not just by chance!
In the mountains, they want snow
Plus, wind that helps snow to blow!

Farmers complain it is now too wet;
Writing poetry is what I suggest!
In the winter, farmers have time;
This also helps poetry to rhyme!

Writing and reading is timely
Helping people with creativity!
Our minds find this so stimulating
Rain needs both believing and timing!

So today I will do more rain dancing
To help the plants that are drying!
Thereafter will come poetry writing
These may be ready for reading!

My own two books were published:
Creative Beyondering[4] is one to read!
Then a novel that is for you Iowans:
Connecting Asians and Americans!

Hopefully these will both be helpful
Reading these may make your mindful!
With winter coming, be prepared
After finishing, they can be shared!

Do not blame me for staying up late!
They may even help you to stay awake!
Winter will go faster with good reading
You may find these books very revealing!

WHY is RAIN so VITAL?

What would we do without rain?
Well, life would never be the same!
Plants, trees and life would shrivel!

Due to the need for more than drizzle!
Rain is so essential for life to grow!
But rain needs the winds to blow!

Mercury and Venus are very hot!
Mars once had rivers we can plot!
Then it became so cold, water froze!

---

[4] Op.cit., 2019, Creative Beyondering, McNaughton Books.

H2O evaporated so could not ooze!
Earth is privileged like Goldilocks!
Not too hot or cold, but just right!

Rain gives rise to civilizations![5]
As water composes 80% of bodies!
Rain provides us with our balance!

As moisture is needed with reliance!
The cycles of seasons are helpful!
Water as rain, snow, ice as H20!

Without rain, civilizations demise!
Because life could not then survive!
Only primitive bacteria maybe alive!

Without rain very little can thrive!
This predicament needs attention!
Now let us consider a real solution!

This poet has learned a remedy!
Seven facets involve real complexity!
If you want to master this, be ready!

First, a group must gather quickly!
Because you need 20-24 in a circle!
Sitting in the dark around a fire!

Four rub lightening rocks together!
To display "quakes" like in a storm!
Four more need big rocks for thunder!

For colliding like in playing billiards!
Plus, three drummers beating jointly!
While 10-12 rain dancers march quickly!

---

[5] Barnett, C., 2015, <u>Rain: A Natural and Cultural History,</u> Crown Press.

All contributors need coordination!
Of course, it helps with practice sessions!
An audience claps with the drumbeats!

They encourage teams in these meets!
Now you're informed about ingredients!
Except for two classified TOP SECRETS!

Be sure to praise your whole crew!
Others want to learn what to do!
Rain dancing leads to your infamy!

Just take the next steps for reality!
Make your own notes for teaching![6]
Your fame comes from rain-dancing!

TOP SECRETS!

Security clearances now become vital!
These secrets are known to be mutual!
Both are very essential for rain-dancing!

So, pay close attention to be succeeding!
Remember, secrets are not broadcast!
But only revealed to those you trust!

First of all, "You need to believe!"
Or else rain-dancing cannot succeed!
Believing is very, very essentially basic!

Without believing, these efforts waste!
If you are not consistently trustful
All these concerted efforts are futile!

---

[6] Book on Rain-Dancing!

Secondly, the secret of "Timeliness!"
All factors come together in its fullness!
So, watch all of the sky cloud formations!

Plus, very critical are weather predictions!
Believe forecasts of moisture for action!
Then the whole team finds satisfaction!

Rejoice! it starts raining in a day!
You will be rewarded with your pay!
Cups of coffee are then the initial fees!

Successes shall lead to higher raises!
Plus send this poet an email at:
gmiddents@yahoo.co.in

FROM FEELING HELPLESS to HOPEFUL

This coronavirus prompts weariness;
Along with feelings of helplessness![7]
Our own efforts are inadequate;
We search for strength as a magnet!

Hopefully our faith is strengthened;
We can look to God as our Friend!
He is both our Creator and Redeemer;
Plus, we also know He is our Savior!

---

[7] Matthew 5: 42

Yes, our physical health is a key;
　　As very own well-being and vitality!
　　　Keep us in contact with each other;
　　　　In Christ, we are sisters and brothers!
Now let us ponder　　　　　　　↑　*Christ is both ours*
　As we wonder.　　　　　┌────────┘　*Hope and Love*
　　Though hard times,　│　　　　*Given to us*
　　　With quiet rhymes from Above!

RELATIONAL BEINGS

An inherent characteristic of animals
　　Are our propensities to be "relationals!"
Many species inherently do recognize
　　Their own variety without compromise!

This phenomenon is critical for species
　　In order to propagate their progenies!
Often rivalries disguise this tendency
　　For relational efforts among progenies!

Offspring are dependent on parents
　　For protection, nurture and relations!
These connections are very essential
　　So that propagation is for survival!

Relational dynamics are necessary
　　For offspring to learn about empathy!
Most parents protect their progeny!
　　These practices are very necessary.

---

[8] I Corinthians 13.

EUROPEAN CULTURES

There are several European cultures,
That has influenced my awareness.
Western Europeans countries first
Including Swedish and Norwegian.

With an Economics Professor in 1973,
We engaged students in these cultures.
Our hosts were very conscientious
So, these exchanges were precious.

We also visited Denmark and Norway
Paris and Amsterdam on New Year's Day.
They were capable in speaking English
So, we only learned very little Swedish.

My ancestors came from Western Germany
But our own schedule was very inflexible.
But this was followed by other visits
Among them were visits with Swiss.

Zurich is home for the Psychologist Jung;
On study leave, two Professional courses.
Then Rome and Vienna were visited
Broadening what I really appreciated.

Other colleagues became good friends.
These are all Western-based cultures.
Subsequent travels were broader
They were delightful to cover.

These experiences were beneficial,
Interdisciplinary and cross-cultural!
My own teaching was influenced
To do broad education of students.

INTER-DISCIPLINARY

I taught "Violence, Terrorism and Peace" in 1970's.
This was inherently timely for Policy Studies.
Students struggled with multi-disciplinary
So they wrestled with the team studies.

Terrorism erupted in the Middle East!
Daily reports came in news releases.
Learners know when studies are relevant
As they watched for timely informants!

My colleague had United Nations Seminars
We accommodated to new Policy Studies!
This is relevant to broaden education
Students learned to do documentation.

January 1980, I had Jungian Seminars;
These were held in Zurich, Switzerland.
I returned to study in January, 1982,
Before a Sabbatical in Washington, D.C.

III. GLOBAL MISSION CHALLENGES

I focused on "Functions of Enemy-making!"
Initially, this title looked very different;
But it contrasts with Peace-making!
Programs are made plus writing!

I began teaching global policy,
As part of our Policy Studies.
One focus was health care;
Also, upon therapeutic care.

As a Texas Licensed Psychologist
For counseling and as a therapist
Plus "Violence and Terrorism;
And dangers of Communism.

Thereupon, came an opportunity
For more on international policy.
This was a Sabbatical in Washington, D.C.
At the Center for Peace and Public Policy.

My late wife accompanied me.
We all responded very positively.
We did both conferring and learning,
Plus, cultural events that were happening.

Moreover, there are historical sites,
Recognizing famous Statesmen.
Plus, the American treasures
Visitation on one's leisure.

Two Houses of the U.S. Congress,
And famous historical museums.
Musical concerts and visual arts,
And travel assistance in carts.[9]

Washington D.C. is our national Capitol;
Americans are typically very curious.
Both interesting and also serious;
Highly recommended for visitors.

INVITATION to RUSSIA

USA vs. USSR had polarization
During 1950-1988 was high tension.
Two Superpowers with nuclear weapons
Powers with greatly tensed apprehension.

Both vying to dominate the world!
Both had their big flags unfurled!
USSR touted their Red Communism
Vying with America in a collision.

Having been an Air Force Nuclear Officer
I closely watched the tense negotiators.
And having written on "Enemy-Making:"
I hoped for greater nuclear peace-making!

The National Council of Churches,
Made efforts to be arbitrators.
Delegation of Church Leaders
Showing steps to be peacemakers!

---

[9] Arlys, my first wife, suffered from crippling arthritis.

These experiences were beneficial;
Interdisciplinary and cross-cultural!
My own teaching was influenced
For broad education of students.

I began teaching global policy,
As part of our policy studies.
One focus was health care;
Also, upon therapeutic care.

As a Licensed Psychologist,
For Counseling as a Therapist.
Plus "Violence and Terrorism,
And dangers of Communism.

Washington, D.C., our national capital
Most Americans are typically curious
Both interesting and also serious
Highly recommended for citizens.

I wrote chapters on national policy;
Along with a colleague for study.
This recorded these key events,
Usable for future college lectures.

Among the other 250 delegates
Three of us were from Texas.
Hosted by Russia's Government
Plus, the Russian Orthodox Church.

Our visits were very well planned;
Twelve teams differently scheduled.
First, we landed in Moscow, the Capitol
Then the teams each had itineraries.

My teams went to Vladimir-Suzdal
    Initial Capitol for Prince Validmir.
        In 988 A.D., this became his home;
            To establish their new Empire.

        Our team leader arranged for me
      For the Hosts and Guests exchange.
  To dialogue with their own leaders,
And to show we were all appreciators.

We also were hosted in Vladimir
    Named after their first leader.
        These were very cordial affairs
            Facilitating times to share.

        Then our group went to Estonia,
      We landed in their Capitol City
  This small nation on Baltic Sea.
Had Scandinavian influences.

We toured a large Collective Farm;
    Lead the Foreman who could charm,
        On behalf of our group, I thanked him
            Tying a big red bandana as our gift.

        When traveling, I take along bandanas;
      Most people recognize them from Texas.
  Bandanas are so easy to carry along
Better than speaking far too long!

In Moscow in the Kremlin twice
    Once for an opera performance!
        A light opera done far too serious
            It was "The Barber of Seville!"

After touring sites in Moscow,
We were also fed Russian caviar.
We were hosted by Church Leaders
Including their leading Archbishops.

East of Moscow is an Orthodox Center
Two Seminaries and large Churches.
We stood for the Worship Services
Because they do not have pews.

A press conference in the Kremlin
Four Soviet reporters knew English.
This was an informative occasion
So they asked for our observations.

Since my research was on "Enemy-Making"
They found this topic very interesting.
I stood up to make my brief remarks
Immediately, they took my photos.

I identified six functions of enemies:[10]
1st, a political function is used frequently.
Leaders gain both power and control;
Identifying enemies makes leaders bold!

2nd, a psychological function is used often;
We are "superior! Enemies are inferior!
3rd, a sociological function is also bold;
This provides cohesiveness control.

4th, enemies have an economic function;
For making profits and more resources.
5th, enemies have a religious function!
We are "good", and enemies are bad!

---

[10] Middeents, G., 2007, <u>Bridging Fear and Peace: From Bullying to doing Justice,</u> Manipal University Press, India.

6th, enemies provide a media function;
Making headlines about the conflicts!
These six functions provide power!
As citizens often hate more war!

This photo printed in the <u>Moscow News!</u>
Russians knew we were exchanging views.
Later the Russian reporters came to Texas
We then also had very interesting exchanges.

Upon return to our homes in America
There was wide interest and inquiries
New media wanted to have reports
Community groups and Churches.

A. A WINSOME INVITATION and AGONIZING DECISIONS!

Later 1984, another invitation,
As Team Leader of 25 persons!
1986 would prepare for 1988 trip
To celebrate 1000 years of Christianity.

So I accepted this to do planning,
1000 delegates commemorating!
This was preparation in June, 1986.
At the Orthodox Seminary, New York.

First week in New York orientation
Then two weeks as guests of Russians.
For 1000 years in 1988 as Christians,
To know how to deal with questions.

By June, my wife was weakening;
So I struggled while deciding.
I resigned as a Leader for 1988.
It was fitting to not further wait.

Her arthritis was progressing;
So my role was to do caring.
1987, her illness was advancing;
In May, 1988, she was terminating.

Arlys died on May 20th 1988.
Fifty-four years of age that date.
Our Daughter, Son and I cried.
We had many decisions ahead.

Two memorial services were held;
The Church she was Ordained Elder!
Second, the "Home Church" in Iowa.
This was also included her burial!

Her basketball teammates all came!
They were Honorary Pall-Bearers.
I was exhausted with grieving,
Reflected in my words speaking.

The grave visited by classmates;
Recalling Old School Classes;
My Sister. Brother plus mates,
Supportive like our Daughter and Son.

We had a tombstone erected;
Originally ground of family farm.
Our Faith held us steadfast;
Even when we were downcast!

B. INTERNATIONAL CONNECTIONS

Now I was a widower with daughter and son
    In the summer of 1988, my new life begun.
        I participated in a conference in Atlanta;
            Visited my mentor, E. Paul Torrance.

        He was retired from the U. of Georgia;
    He was by this time also a widower.
We appreciated each other deeply
Recalled mutual colleagues admiringly.

Organizational Development Institute
    Offered a study conference in China.
        This was an exciting experience
            That did capture my interest!

        Beijing was our very first meeting;
    Tiananmen Square was compelling.
We visited China's Institute of Health.
We also attended a Chinese Opera.

We flew to the ancient capitol, Xian;
    The field of Ancient Soldiers nearby.
        Constructed over 2000 ago of stone.
        They gave realistic impressions.

        Chinese food was appreciated
    They were all glad that we visited.
Then on to the City of Chunking;
Located high on the Yangtze River

Our Conference was on a Riverboat;
    Cruising through the ROYAL GORGES.
        We stopped for a day in Wuhan;
            Noted now for the coronavirus.

Conferred at Hangzhou University;
I presented a paper on Teamwork!
China had about 200 Psychologists
With keen team-building interests.

Our hosts invited me to do teaching;
We made plans for the next year.
A Psychologist was coming to America;
So, I hosted him on his tour for lectures.

We confirmed plans for the fall of 1989;
I could obtain a new leave-of-absence.
Before the trip, Tiananmen Sq. violence!
Plans were arrested as a consequence.

Hangzhou is a Chinese cultural center.
Today it has expanded even further.
Onward to Shanghai and Tokyo;
I was hosted by a colleague!

My host's son was a teenager;
With his Father at Austin College.
The boy had been with him at five.
Enrolled in Arlys' Kindergarten.

Later he studied at Carleton College!
Then a Doctorate at Wisconsin U.
This family is very respected
As colleagues, very valued!

The Journal of Organizational Behavior,
Published two of my papers I composed.
We met at Maibour University in Slovenia.
Which was a state in old Yugoslavia.

"Constructive Responses by Policy Analysis,"
Was my professional paper that I gave;
Dean Majez Mulej then invited me
To teach at Lhublyana University.

He was invited to the U. of N. Texas,
It hosted an international conference.
I was also giving a paper on teamwork;
So we blended interests and hosted him.

Dr. Majez Mulej was a Marxist Economist;
He was the international global expert.
I was asked to then introduce him;
The 450 in the audience listened.

He asked them two quick questions:
"What is your most important asset?"
He suggested: "Your Human Resources!"
Then he proceeded to provide support.

The next year, Yugoslavia disintegrated;
My invitation had to go through Belgrade.
This experience was therefore cancelled
International invitations again limited.

PROFESSIONAL PUBLICATIONS of 1990's:

"PSYCHOLOGICAL PERSPECTIVES on ENEMY-MAKING,"
ORGANIZATIONAL DEVELOPMENT JOURNAL,
Summer !990.
"ORGANIZATIONAL DEVELOPMENT in PRACTICE
TEACHING."

A Pilot Course on "Psychology Applied to the
Workplace." ORGANIZATIONAL DEVELOPMENT
JOURNAL. Fall, 1990.
Books Written and Published:
CRISIS in VIOLENCE and PEACE,
Manipal University, India, 1998.

C. BROADER CHALLENGES

We cannot yet know, but we pretend
Imagining life's beginning and the end!
What propels us to go on this pursuit?
Inward energy? Or upward as a recruit?

Military personnel are "Called Up!"
To serve our nation in its interests!
Ministers have their own holy calling!
Plus, dedicated people who are answering!

These callings typically are challenging!
Going to assignments that are inviting!
Prompting persons to pursue their destiny
As essential actors in these earthly dramas!

Many calls have common cores!
One is the call that invites us to serve!
Human needs are most everywhere
With necessities needing us to share!

Employed persons are called to serve!
Cultures benefit from becoming involved!
Service is among the worthy callings
To activities that result in benefiting!

When one's gifts match human needs!

This combination hopes to succeed!
Successes in something significant!
Leads into service that is important!

Serving is one of the helping careers!
That is fulfilling among one's peers!
Facilitating the aspirations of others
Quickly become sisters and brothers!

Police, homemakers, business persons
Plus, our teachers, clergy and nurses!
Benefits from constructive activities;
Contributing to human beneficiaries!

In drama-"The World is Our Stage!"
"Psycho-drama" draws likes a page.
Each participant expresses their role
Spontaneous contributors with a soul!

Imagine how future living will unfold!
Will some be brave and others bold?
Or might be regression back to ages old?
Backward comforts! vs. forward untold?

Let us imagine we choose our role!
As persons participating on this globe!
What destiny becomes our experience?
Capturing our now unknown existence?

Existential issues then confront us!
Courageous or cowardly in our face?
Life unfolds like a drama on stage!
Will each express us in the new age?

Homo sapiens have brief existence!
Other creatures have been patients!

Humans assume a predominant role!
     Is this real or an illusion from old?

Human recently learned languages!
     That enlarges us into linguistic ages!
Do other species have their own minds?
     Do humans have the humility to learn?

Researchers discover that species talk!
     Helpful to know in this linguistic age!
Communicating for mates and empathy!
     Whales and elephants do this already!

Will this species reach another step?
     To appreciate planetary creatures?
Mutual respect will become essential
     Facilitating universal new languages!

Foreign beings may seem as arrogant!
     Like an ideal model to then interact!
We presume to be the intellectuals
     New actors wonder about our worth!

Will our Divinities be theirs' also?
     Challenging our Creator as universal?
In a 1000 years, much will be learned!
     Previously we may have even spurned!

Diverse requests come to us to serve!
     Invitations may be explicit or disguised!
Calls involve doing clear functions!
     Often this may involve offering provisions!

Fulfilling important human needs!
     Essential to nature and vital deeds!
Calls to be a very entrusted person!
     To deliver vital services to someone!

Performing important duties is involved!
 These are necessary for being called!
Watch for opportunities for service!
 Simple tasks or elected to public office!

Encouraging is very often a vital calling!
 Honoring perspectives others are having!
Listening to viewpoints can be relieving!
 Providing an outlet others are needing!

"Expectograms" vary widely in callings!
 So, our sensitivity is essential in serving!
The needs of humans require flexibility!
 A key helpful gift known as creativity!

INVITED into the FUTURE

Is humanity now prepared to go ahead?
 Or might many be reluctant instead?
Adventures need major mutual support!
 As Columbus and Pilgrims making efforts!

Humans are curious about "The Endgame!"
 Will it lead to defeat or perhaps to fame?
Adventurous callings have many unknowns
 More than mathematics with formulas shown!

More is needed than beliefs in the future!
 Faith and trust are essential in this venture!
Anchors beyond human knowledge are needed!
 For upholding humanity in order to succeed!

Future demands new human creativity!
 Humanity will require even more originality!

Old methods will need additional mobility!
  Even beyond each century after century!

Next millennium has mysterious uncertainties!
  Prompting awesome wonderments for humanity!
Faith and Science are anchors for personalities!
  But an eye-blink as humans now await eternity!

The future is unknown to us now!
  Above and below; sideways not out!
Ahead is hazy, unclear and risky!
  Foreboding, unexplored and "iffy!"

Forward goes just around the corner!
  Unfolding seconds, minutes and hours!
Forecasts are percentage probabilities
  Projected straight ahead for possibilities!

The reality in living requires confidence!
  Proceeding ahead with considerable trust!
To be ready as the future is realized!
  Aware that we will likely be surprised!

RISK-TAKING

Living now and in the future is risky!
  This is true with so many uncertainties!
Early humans faced grave insecurities
  The next 1000 years had many mysteries!

Doing nothing does not assure safety!
  Foolish risks increase shorter longevity!
Risk-taking can be calculated scientifically
  Expressed mathematically in probabilities!

Such calculations are useful pragmatically!
  Statistics are helpful in projecting futurities!
Some wise plans can be made realistically!
  So that greater safety is made for humanity!

Life provides choices to become faithful!
  Giving assurance that we can be trustful!
God made provisions by sacrificing His Son!
  Redeeming believers to live into the Beyond!

Our lives have numerous interruptions!
  Unpredicted and without anticipations!
Little interruptions do small interferences:
  Telephone, door knocks and preferences!

But major interruptions may be upsetting!
  Disruptions require do difficult changing!
Our routines then are no longer flowing!
  Changing course from where we are going!

God's Calling to us demands our attention!
  Expecting change without full comprehension!
For preparing to undertake new direction!
  Responding faithfully with apprehension!

God is hoping that we will be responsive!
  Rather than stubborn with resistance!
Our calling may require preparation
  Making demands in these interruptions!

EXAMPLES

Abram and Sarah called from Ur of Chaldees[11]
    "To go" with only a few unclear promises!
Moses and wife were disrupted in Median!
    To be concerned for treatment by Egyptians!

Old Testament prophets heard callings!
    To warn God's People who were falling!

John the Baptist[12] made calls to repent!
    Because God's People had become bent!

Jesus' call is explained in St. Luke 4.
    To help the poor and release prisoners!
Announcing acceptance of God's Kingdom!
    To deliver the New Gospel of "The Word!"

Ordinary persons were called as Disciples!
    Changing their labors to become Followers!
Saul [13]was struck down traveling to Damascus!
    Changed to Paul as Christ's own witness!

Invitations to become Christ's Messengers
    In whatever field where we are workers!
These disruptions have Divine Purpose!
    To demonstrate Christ's Gospel on earth!

Early Christians had their lives changed!
    Subsequent responders also contributed!
Devoted to Jesus as their new Savior!
    To share the Good News without favor!

---

[11] Genesis 11:
[12] Luke 3: 1-20
[13] Acts 9:

Christians carried forth as witnesses!
With their human limits and excesses!
Reformers insisted on difficult changes!
Enlarging the outreach of the Churches!

Women and men, youth and children
Become adherents and also Pilgrims!
In work, play, school and communities
Wherever they may discover opportunities!

RESPONDING

The Callings of Christ continues today!
Inviting us followers to share "The Way!"
Reaching outward is also the challenge!
To discover avenues to be "Evangels!"

Our calling is now as our "vocation!"
Responding positively in our occupations!
To be "advocates" of Christ's Good News!
Centering our lives and sharing His Views!

Yes, His Calling may be an interruption!
In our personal agendas as a disruption!
Determination may be needed to obey
Persisting as we follow "Christ's Way!"

Yes, we face risks to carry through!
We are not along in whatever we will do!
Christ is with us for sharing "Good News!"
This promise persists to share His Views!

Beyond "success" proceeding to significance
"Significant Successes" expand our experiences!
Contributing by addressing further involvements!
Involving persons to engage in "Beyonderments!"

DISCOVERING OUR CALLING!

"Calling" is elegantly described!
Where are needs are in the world?
Match your own personal gifts!
This serves up what is a shift!

Further guidance can be discovered
Four facets [14]compose a call from God!
First, is His Invitation to discipleship!
This is basic before analyzing your gifts!

Secondly, is your personal awareness
"Your Secret Call" gives you guidance!
This is unique your own individually!
Inviting you to set forth personally!

A third factor involves your qualities,
Do you possess now or develop abilities?
Expected of a candidate to be educated
In order to acquire skills that are expected!

Fourthly, a call comes from the Church![15]
You are needed, prepared and available!
This is a confirmation of the prior stages
Matching your gifts to fulfill ministries!

---

[14]   Johnson, 1967 Yale University Dean in a personal communication while both served on a committee for assessing standards exams for ordination in the UPC USA.

[15]   Book of Order, Presbyterian Church, USA.

Calling and Clarity[16] *is a very good book!*
  Discovering What God Wants for Your Life.
This provides broader grasp for Christians
  Designed to guide one's personal decisions!

A person may feel overwhelmed in searching
  Considering hopes and limitations is confusing!
Examining one's skills, loves & community
  Plus, cultural expectations and one's identity!

There are no adequate vocational algorithms!
  For us to respond to God's own invitations!
Profound Truths about oneself is needed
  Assisting all persons on how to proceed!

"Missional Calling" hears the Voice of God!
  What God wants done in this broken world!

This is a "relational theology of calling!"
  By asking personally: "Who is the Caller?"

Wrestling will sustain ones' own obedience
  In our commitment with spiritual disciplines!
Personal counseling may add clarification
  As a person makes these serious decisions!

---

[16]   Koskela, D (2015) Calling and Clarity: Discovering What God Wants for Your Life, Eerdmanns.

IV. MARVELOUS INTRODUCTION

After a sad period of family grieving
I re-started to go out venturing!
My family and friends did help
Connecting with new people!

In Fall 1988, travel was possible;
I joined a "Global Organization."
I had a Sabbatical for a semester
So, I signed up for a new adventure.

A global conference going to China;
With 25 new members as collegial;
We met first in San Francisco
Then flew across the Pacific!

We then conferred in Beijing;
China had very few Psychologists.
Then onward to the city of Xian,
Saw 1000's stone historic soldiers.

Our main conference was in Chunking;
This historically famous interior city.
Boarded a River Boat on Yangtze
We conferred with colleagues.

Viewing the "Royal Gorges!"
Stone walls for 100's of miles.
We stopped in the City of Wuhan[17]
Intensely crowded market streets.

---

[17] In 2019, the contagious coronavirus originated.

Then traveled to Hangzhou University
Conferring their Chinese Faculties!
My professional paper presented:
"Evaluating Teamwork by Members!"[18]

Introduced to their Department Chair;
He had a leave to study in America.
I was invited to be a Visiting Professor
To teach a Hangzhou U. in 1990.

As a single widow, I was ready to go;
But riots in Tiananmen Square, Beijing.
My invitation was cancelled to China;
They needed to deal with problems.

Teaching at Austin College continued;
My son, Greg, lived also in Sherman.
We shared the family house jointly;
I continued as a member of Rotary!

Summer, 1990, six colleagues went to Africa;
Designed to broaden International Studies.
Old historic Egypt included archeology.
This Included sites noted Biblically.

Then across the Sahara go Ghana;
Slave deportation site near Accra.
Onward to an interior city of Kumasi
Invited to speak at meeting of Rotary.

When I finished, two Rotarians asked:
"Can we ask you a personal question?"
I replied: "Sure, just go on to ask:"
"How old are you?" requested.

---

[18] Middents, G., published in <u>Journal of Organizational Psychoogy.</u>

"I'm 58 years," I then replied.
One poked the other and said:
"See I told you, he is not 85!"
Yes, my own white hair misled!

"He couldn't make this trip at 85!"
So, they saw I was still alive!
Yes, my buddy, Tom Nuckols
And I had a big chuckle!

Then back to Cairo, Egypt,
Visited Church of Christians.
About nine million members,
Tolerated by Egyptian Muslims.

Back to Texas for the Fall Term;
We educated students in turn.
Africa is a prime continent,
Global education important!

TALENT of MATCHMAKERS!

In the Fall of 1990, a new experience;
By my former Secretary, Margaret.
She served twenty years earlier
Then she worked in Dallas.

Margaret knew a single woman
She knew I was a widower man.

"Would you like to meet Carol Ann?"
She knew her at work and me as a man.

"Yes," I affirmed with my response;
So, I was given her telephone number!
In early November, I called Carol Ann
We made a date with mutual plans.

What a fortunate experience for me!
I had been a widower over 30 months.
She lived in Dallas; I lived in Sherman
I discovered she is a very fine woman!

In late 1990, an exciting experience!
I met my marvelous new mate!
Carol Ann and I had our date!
We visited an Art Museum.

Then she took me to dinner!!
Honoring her Lutheran Minister!
She was President of a large church;
Plus, she is also dedicated to her work.

We had a marvelous time dating!
Met in Sherman<>Dallas traveling.
Our colleagues also became aware
That we were learning to share.

Visiting Santa Fe has also continued!
During summer months to be renewed!
Back in 1988, I then became a widower.

Five years later, Carolann is my "Wifer!"
I proposed on St. Francis Hotel veranda!
This quaint place was perfect for my song!

What Are You Doing the Rest of Your Life?
Barbra Streisand

What are you doing the rest of your life
        North and South and East and West of your life
I have only one request of your life
        That you spend it all with me!

All the seasons and the times of your days
        All the nickels and the dimes of your days
Let the reasons and the rhymes of your days
        All begin and end with me!

I want to see your face in every kind of light
        In fields of gold and forests of the night
And when you stand before the candles on a cake
        Let me be the one to hear the silent wish you make!

Those tomorrows waiting deep in your...
        Those tomorrows waiting deep in your eyes
In a world of love you keep in your eyes
                I'll awaken what's asleep in your eyes

It may take a kiss or two through all of my life
        Summer, winter, spring and fall of my life
            All I ever will recall of my life!

After joyously accepting my proposal
We worshiped at St. Francis Cathedral!
During our evening dinner, another surprise!

She discovered her St. Francis necklace medal!
The Hispanic legend gave her assurance
That within a year, a promise for marriage!

So, St. Francis is very significant to us!
His prayer included in wedding service!
The world now has Pope St. Francis!

His joyous image is now with all of us!
Carolann and I plan a September Trip
To Rome, West Turkey and to Greece!

Will we have a St. Francis audience?
Maybe you can provide us assistance!
We would welcome any of your efforts!

That would broaden our own horizons!
We could also tell him or New Mexico!
Plus, Ghost Ranch and also Santa Fe!

CAROL ANN's CAREER

Carol is a successful business woman!
Serving as Vice-President of Board Affairs.
Her corporate skills are magnificent!
At the Cornerstone Credit Union!

Over 700 Credit Unions as members;
Compose of over seven million members.
Her communication skills are noteworthy!
Covering Texas, Arkansas and Oklahoma!

Our marriage is nearly three decades!
She has traveled with me abroad!
First to Switzerland in Europe
As I taught a Jungian Course.

Then she went with me to India!
The first trip to New Delhi and Nepal!
We rested in a mountain area camp;
Then to Kathmandu near Mt. Everest.

In 1998, Carol joined me in Kerala, India!
Coming by herself to land in Kochi, Kerala!
I was invited to teach at UC College
She addressed the young women!

In 2001, I was at Manipal University!
During 9/11—attack of New York City!
Ten weeks later, she bravely flew again
To join me in late 2001 coming to Manipal.

Rotarians requested we join a medical mission;
First, we traveled to India inoculating children.
Polio soon was eradicated in all of India;
Then we also flew onward to Viet Nam.

Young children and teens had hopes;
That we be would adopt as their parents.
Girls gravitated to Carol to get attention!
Many children have come to the United States.

This prompted me to write a new novel:
<u>Connecting Asians and Americans!</u>
Inter-relatedness is badly needed;
Vietnamese children are adopted.

Carol has become the joy of my life!
She is a blessing to have as my wife!
We mutually enjoy one another
My family knows her better!

My Daughter and Son are joyed!
Two Granddaughters have rejoiced!
Our larger families are very pleased;
We share Faith and Goals we shared.

We live in Dallas on Burgundy Road,
This comfortable house is our home.
Convenient on this urban location;
Now I will share my appreciation:

BOOK PUBLISHED IN 2007:
BRIDGING FEAR and PEACE: From Bullying to Doing
Justice, Manipal University Press, 2007.

Carol Appreciated by Appreciator

Just let me get carried away deeply within my heart,
Before I get into other writing to make another start!
I profoundly appreciate you more in every way!
I want to write this explicitly beyond what I say!

Intuitively beyond what you tell me, you have stress,
Inherently you have learned how to handle this press!
People know they can count on you to make delivery,
As you have decades of experience done confidently.

Now whatever your work has on your agenda today,
You even are magnanimous when people are cranky!
You are very conscientious to do whatever it takes,
Since your experiences do things for others' sakes!

We had a splendid weekend doing interesting things,
While parlaying your own energy while that guy sings!
Our meals extended into meals for us to enjoy today,
Plus washing clothes that did not even smell anyway!

Don't be surprised if cohorts are crabby on Monday!
Starting a busy week may not be what to do preferably.
Fragile egos particularly require special time and care,
Some might be cantankerous in contaminating the air!

Remember our home front where you are appreciated,
Others may have a bad weekend, or even constipated!
Don't let them ruffle your feathers or make you a tizzy,
Keep your eye on goals to make a straight furrow easy

INVITATION to VOLUNTEERING[19]

Volunteering becomes very fulfilling!
Your services to people who are waiting!
They may have a range of serious needs;
Both domestically and also overseas.

A variety of skills can be volunteered!
Matching your expertise to those needed!
Children, youth, adults and also elderly,
Need assistance delivered very personally!

Both medical care and basic nursing!
Even broader are schools and teaching!
Agricultural skills can fulfill actions!
Plus, new technology for applications!

---

[19]   Presbyterian Church World Mission

Volunteering demands personal courage!
Offering your services without subsidies!
Compensation comes from satisfactions
Investing ourselves with determination!

Addressing needs is personally fulfilling!
Both tangibly and intangibly as rewarding!
Affirmed personally my own services!
Consulting in Poland, China, Slovenia![20]

A. NEW ERA with CAROL ANN!!!

Serving six months twice to teach in India:[21]
1998 to plan a graduate degree in Psychology.
During 2001, filling a University Peace Chair,
As Professor at the very large Manipal University.

Lecturing at nine sub-colleges on Peace and Justice
Plus Polio Plus [22]*inoculation for children in 2004!*
Then a new medical mission into Vietnam;
And later for creating interfaith seminars!

In March, 2016, Carol Ann and I,
Went to volunteer in Nicaragua!
With two groups of Rotarians,
Including Young College Students.

---

[20]   Invitation to World Congresses of Organizational Development Institute.

[21]   Invitation by Principal Thomas John, Prof. Of Psychology, Union Christian College affiliated with Mahatma Gandhi University in 1998; In 2001, an Invitation to fill UNESCO Endowed Peace Chair, Manipal University during Aug.-December of 2001.

[22]   Invitation by Governor of Rotary International, District 5810, Pete Synder to join a team of Rotarians from Middle America.

Now developing Science<>Religion exchanges,
Drawing people to share their perspectives!
Satisfaction comes with participating;
Feedback emerges that is encouraging!

YOU CAN DO IT!

Our young grandnephew at eight years,
Helped my wife learn some new skills!
She was shooting basketball to score!
Uncertain just how to push the ball!

Little Craig gave genuine encouragement:
"You Can Do It!" was his clear comment!
His advice was full of assistance and hope!
She still remembers this as an Executive!

When God Calls us "You Can Do It!"
Let's not ignore or say we cannot!
Yes, major effort is typically needed
Without this, whoever succeeded?

Rewards are both tangible and intangible!
Unless we really try, it is not manageable!
Sure, not everything works automatically!
Undertaking callings to be done faithfully!

If you are in search for meaningful living,
You can discover you are important to God!
Then if you let God be important to you!
Your meaning in life you can pursue!

God is calling now for you to help!
Serving Him where's there need!
"When you do what you love,
Everything else falls in place!"

SUMMER CONFERENCES

In recent decades, we attended conferences!
Staying for a week at the Ghost Ranch!
This original dude ranch is also lovely!

Surrounded by mountains charmingly!
Georgia O'Keefe did many paintings
Capturing nature's panorama for art.

Our children enjoyed living on a ranch,
With wide-open trails to also roam!
They loved the horses to rider upon!

Our memories remind us of pleasures
For weeks in the mountain treasures!
Learning of how Indian lived earlier!

People from all over this country,
Participated with us pleasantly!
Conferences had excellent leaders!

To stretch our minds as learners!
Our Church sponsored conferences
Addressing many interesting topics!

CAROL's QUALITIES

Carol brings people readily together!
She is obviously a key facilitator!
Moreover, she is a keen manager;
As her husband, her appreciator!

Connecting people is one of her skills!
On Corporation Boards, all can fulfill.
On Church Committees, she urges service,
With all ages, she motivates their purpose!

Moreover, she brings diversity into focus;
Including gender, race, age and experience.
She knows how to facilitate communication,
So that persons work jointly toward action!

She accepted an invitation to Kenya!
Her team trained persons from 5 nations.
Her cross-cultural skills are very apparent;
She was asked to return another time.

Carol drives when I am invited to Churches;
Sometimes she also helps in the worship!
People quickly become appreciative;
It is apparent she has natural gifts!

An unusual request was made in India:
Church Members asked us to sing a duet!
So, we selected a very familiar hymn;
This added to making our contribution!

MORE THAN BIOLOGICAL

Most obvious features are biological!
  But hidden propensity of relational!
Protecting offspring is indispensable!
  Both physically and also to be sociable!

Relational is a learned phenomenon
  Contrast to what is biologically human!
These relations became "compassional:"
  Plus what is called cognitively rational!

Along with compassion is empathy
  This is an inherent human quality!
These qualities are also emotional
  Combining the emotions with rational!

PERSONAL

These verses express my own personal:
  Like most people, I learned from familial!
My parents were caring and compassionate
  My own older siblings also were empathic!

My childhood was typically nurturing
  Expressed also by my two siblings!
While there were few disagreements
  These were resolved within moments!

Relational experiences are combined
  From bio-physical and also psycho social!
These complex occurrences are valued
  Undergirded by faith that is relational!

The Great Commandment guides us:
Love God and love your neighbor!
My neighbors are local and globally
With compassionate relationally!

Fortunately, I also learn from mates;
My first wife was a school classmate!
As Mother of our daughter and son,
Dying at 54 while still very young!

Providentially, I meet my second wife
Who has now become the joy of my life!
I am grateful that we were introduced;
Now for 28 years we are married!

Daughter and husband have two daughters!
My son is another joy is still a bachelor!
Joyfully, they have are learned empathy!
Along with compassion relationally!

In multi-disciplinary fields about people
I constantly have learning experiences!
As a Minister and also a Psychologist
Interpersonal relations, I am blest!

My own personal reflections are joyful!
These are both joyful and meaningful!
My Faith in God comes thru Jesus Christ
Sustaining me on my journey in my life!

Wholeness is both emotional and cognitive!
Rather than separately compartments!
Moreover, life is relational and spiritual,
Synthesized together to be integral!

INDIVIDUAL <> COMMUNITY

Individualism is highly valued!
 Advancing a person as privilege d!
  Honoring freedom to engage in action!
   Helping an individual for infraction!

   This viewpoint is typically American!
  Contrasted with community protection!
Nations that value their own society,
Because individuals are secondary!

Freedom is primary for individuals
 To exercise their own opportunities!
  This position is valued in free states
   Who honor each person in debates!

EXCESSES

A person prefers to be unrestricted!
 In order to pursue what is preferred!
  Rules and regulations are for others!
   Not a person who does their druthers!

   Doing your thing is licentiousness!
  Identified by strict religious codes!
What considerations for societies?
When there are fights and conflicts?

If one is able to do their thing,
 Others might become victims!
  What recourse is available?
   So, settlements are equitable?

When actions are irresponsible
Is there equity in this system?
If a perpetrator has freedom?
Those injured are victims!

For example, who gets a gun?
Is this limited to only some?
Should everyone own a gun?
Would safety be for everyone?

B. HOW THEN SHALL WE LIVE?

What is an optimal arrangement?
So that each person is protected!
Could this system be perfect?
So, freedom<>collective persist?

What about one is a burglar?
Or rampant mass murderer?
How would there be controls?
To protect persons and souls?

Are morals and religion enough?
So that global people may prosper?
These are not easy to quickly solve;
As our human history shows!

How were laws to get enacted?
Who were those to be protected?
Everyone or only the privileged?
Would violations be punished?

How would justice be enacted?
As fairness is implemented!
So, all parties are protected
And violations investigated?

Social consensus is essential!
So, differences are legislated!
Judges and juries are selected
And witnesses are interrogated!

Procedural justice is necessary!
Understandable and published
Plus, consistently practiced
All citizens are protected!

C. WHY MORE?

Doing "More" with less is an important key to future sustainability,
　　Our human propensity for "more" is exhausting creation's capacity.
"More" appeals to our weakness to accumulate with greediness,
　　What are root causes motivating "more" possessions and sleaziness?

Acquiring acquisitions insidiously leads to pursuing acquirements,
　　The pleasure of possessing abundance is our selfish inheritances.
Hunger for good nourishment is basic for assuring human survival,
　　If others control what we want to have they are considered a rival.

Hasty skirmishes understandably occur to satisfy to our appetites,
　　Dominant control provides ready access to what we can accumulate.
Aggressive individuals become honored heroes to then be recognized,
　　National standing armies provide the soldiers who are fully armed.

No wonder that warring tribes become increasingly more aggressive,
Scarcities critically motivate people to become more possessive.
Accumulations of essential resources compounds human selfishness,
"Controlling goodies" promotes more vulnerability to greediness.

Acquisitions take many forms from food to land to jewels and money,
Often levels of wealth typically prompt envy so that one has plenty!
Does this analysis provide clues about dynamics to accumulate "more?"
So, tribes multiply into expansive nations going from shore to shore!

Middle agents specialize in trading commodities in order to gain profits,
Facilitating trade as banks loan money for sellers to reach markets.
The astute commercial traders cultivate customers whom "they serve:"
Products, real estate, labor, services and transportation resources.

Opportunities, training experiences, partnerships and corporations,
Cartels, holding companies, stock markets, brokers and financiers.
Accumulating acquirements of land or real estates and commodities,
Globalization prompts both contrasts of macro-micro-economics.

What does motivate these activities so that people become obsessed?
Do these pre-occupations transform to both occupations and fields?
Then courses and degrees advance careers into varieties of marketing,
Major resources are accumulated into "More and More Coveting!"

Promoting More-"isming"

Marketing magazines advance the special interests of entrepreneurs,
"MORE" is the title that captures the incentives for "more-galore!"
Advertising introduces potential consumers to purchase even more,
From all fashions, adornments, vehicles, consumer goods in stores.

Business bachelors and master degrees now known to be "MBA's,"
　　The graduates become masters who specialize into profitable ways.
Aggressive marketers invade Wall Street, religion and even health care,
　　By manipulating transactions so brokers, they get a very big share!

This financial acumen can quantitatively become big complications,
　　In fact, few criminal investigations can comprehend transactions.
Yes, Business Ethics has been introduced to engender more trust,
　　Dubious enforcement and "self-regulations" make ethics a must!

While regulations and laws are designed to punish criminal acts,
　　Cunning psychopaths can find illegal methods to cloud true facts,
Then the naïve persons who assumes every one regulates themselves,
　　Exploit innocent persons are unaware and vulnerable to thieves.

Because we brought nothing into this world, we can take nothing out![23]
　　If we have food and clothing, we will be content and then not pout![24]
Those wanting riches are trapped into temptation by senselessness,
　　Plus, harmful desires that plunge us into ruin and distrustfulness!

Loving money is a root of all kinds of evil and likewise human desires,
　　Eagerness to be rich prompts wandering away from their own faith!
They "pierce themselves with many pains" and also waste personally,
　　If everyone exploited each other, nature would be more unsustainable!

Our challenge as "civilized people" we need to "do more with less!"
　　We are coming into "an age of anxiety" that requires resourcefulness.
We have been seduced by big corporate profits and personal wealth,
　　"MORE" possessions, "MORE" merchandizing and "MORE" health!

---

[23] St. Paul, I Timothy 6:7 in the <u>New Testament of the Bible</u> "For we brought nothing into this world, so that we can take nothing out of it!"

[24] <u>Ibid.,</u> verses 6:8 "But if we have food and clothing we will be content with these!"

This quest for riches is now recognized as fostering unethical behavior,
    Research by Daniel Piff[25] and others to breaks the law while driving.
Plus exhibiting more unethical decision-making tendencies for wealth,
    And take valued goods and property from others who are innocent.

Behavioral research also reveals that the upper class lies in negotiations,
    They also tend to cheat to increase their chances for winning prizes!
Endorsing unethical behavior also occurs at work for their selfish gain,
    This confirms hypotheses upper-class persons have tendencies
    to greed.

There are indications that wealthy persons are practicing "solipsism,"
    They apparently assume that what they do everyone should copy.
This reinforces their thinking in a circular form of self-affirmation,
    Assuming that others should see their role like their confirmation.

Our challenge as "civilized people" we now need to do more with less!
    We are coming into "an age of scarcity" that takes resourcefulness.
We have been seduced by personal and corporate profits and wealth,
    Plus "MORE" possessions for selfish greed that is not social health.

Gone are making things, but rather "MORE" super markets and goods,
    We now want "MORE" cars, "MORE" highways, "MORE" rich foods!
Hooked on MORE of everything, MORE supermarkets and big stores,
    MORE crops per acre, MORE oil and gas, MORE government
    programs.

History has also made previous revelations: "This works until it doesn't!"
    We have become addicted to "MORE" but now we also need to learn,
In weaning ourselves from our possessions, now we cannot be careless,
    We must embrace a "a Spirit of competitive frugality in service
    of less!

---

[25] Piff, Paul, el.al., 2012 "Higher Social Class Predicts Increased Unethical Behavior,"

Doing "MORE with less" must become both our mantra and our motto,
Becoming savers, we may become more inventive and more
diplomatic.
The "Era of Abundance," "of Growth," "Wastes" are definitely enigmatic,
Competitive prudence requires less water and carbon, creating
less magic!

"Lost time is never found again" was Benjamin Franklin's old saying,
Natural resources and fossil fuels lost to what we now are
discovering.
These survives after what has been learned has long been forgotten,
This requires unlearning old excuses using B.F. Skinner's new
education.

The Enemy of Individualism
is Group Think[26]

Gates helped establish Black Studies as a Professor at Harvard University,
He is widely known in the United States since his reputation is
scholarly.
Popular press amplified his notoriety in the White House Beer Garden,
With both President Obama and Officer Crowley who had
arrested him.

While perplexed and displeased with that 15-minute photo "smoozing,"
He optimizes this impact with his writing and lecturing and teaching.
Pioneering the awareness of racially diverse perspectives in being black,
His insights penetrate Western history of slavery from a long
way back!

---

[26] Louis, Henry, April 18k, 2011, "Skip Gates, Jr., and Holds Everyone Accountable,"
Newsweek. And Lisa Miller, pp. 42-45, "Skip Gates Next Big Idea."

One of his aphorisms: "The Enemy of Individualism is Group Think!"
    While provocative, it begs for clarification in order to understand.
Enemy-making has unconscious dynamics known also as projection,
    Each polarity blames the other side in complicating more opposition.

Americans prize freedom of individual expression over tribal loyalty,
    While the larger social group receives less secondary tribal fealty.
This opposition is reflected in surface expressions of scapegoating,
    Blaming the other polarity as scope goats then is openly happening.

But in unconscious projection, each party is unaware of its hatred,
    In fact, denying hostility shows up in early stages before divorced.
A mate may begin to have negative perceptions of the other mate,
    If disenchantment may gradually build up, it then may be too late.

In previous superpower struggles between the East and the West,
    Hatred and fear built up into Mutually Assured Destruction(MAD).
The Soviets projected their own internal hatred upon Americans,
    Likewise, Americans saw in the Soviets their own denied anger.

At the political plane, democratic elections have room for individuals,
    Increasingly in primary elections, entrepreneurial candidates declare.
Individual promote their own campaign with media amplifications,
    These persons then seek support in a popularity contest for positions.

While political parties have a major role in multiplying popularity,
    Party disciplines shaping their group think has been reduced noticeably.
Winners take legislative office, while subordinating themselves to others,
    Coalitions are testy, but so are joint decisions in how to be collaborators.

Jury procedures by citizens clearly require group think to reach decisions,
  Judges may function individually while Supreme Courts are groupers.
In order to reach their verdict, collaborative decisions are essential,
  As individual Judges who make their own decisions to rule in trials.

Members of legislative branches are losing teamwork collaboration,
  So many individuals see stardom in order to gain media coverage.
They may become individual stars who want for also predominance,
  But they are expected to submerge their egos to strengthen influence.

Overall, these self-perpetuating practices to seeking more to accumulate,
  Is one of selfish characteristic of what is known as the human species.
This motivation to "ACQuire MORE" is at the core of basic dilemmas,
  Without sharing in the common good, human existence is tentative.

PROBLEM-SOLVING

We are faced with social issues!
  Needing skills in social practices!
    Defining the problems is necessary
      Rather than starting with solutions!

      Are these social issues in civility?
    Who will be involved officially?
  Researching alterative systems
Covering the entire community!

After thorough analysis of input,
  From both social practices and laws,
    Plus, values and religious positions
      And likewise cultural traditions!

Gathering data is significant
Including legal precedence!
Consult citizens and leaders!
Identify the best alternatives!

After analyzing the problem
Then developing alternatives!
Cross-examining their strengths
While identifying weaknesses!

Prioritizing is another step
Then selected what is best!
Careful editing and brevity,
Ready for media publicity!

Sharing with decision-makers.
Suggesting possible legislation!
Answering relevant questions
And anticipating objections!

To solve community problems
Fair to a person and collective!
With proposal for legislature!
Urge decision to be cooperative!

Wide consensus is preferable
For implementation readily!
Educate society very widely
Important for all humanity!

Identify fair time for evaluation!
Expectations to make revisions!

Improving the implementation,
Of the widest population!

Questioning and Answering

What occurs between the occasion when questions
*   are posed and answer discovered?*
Is there contemplation and reflection? What then
*   happens in the mind of the question?*
The other side, how do questions affect the
*   hearers inquire when put on the spot.*
Arenas between Q&A is the focus of these verses
*   where people where battles are fought?*

How do you respond as these five interrogatories are
*   now posed directly to you for answers.?*
Inside yourself as you ponder, numerous brain neurons
*   and gut reactions may be registered.*
"Caught in the Middle is the No-Man's Land" where
*   you can be shot by more adversaries.*
Are you on the defensive to protect yourself;
*   you have an offense to respond quickly.*

In the dialogues that follow, "Q" stands for
*   "Questioner" while "A" for those answering,*
While exploring from childhood to seniority,
*   humans have developmental games evolving.*
While a fetus is in their Mother's womb, Parents
*   typically have many questions to ask:*
When will this baby arrive? Is it a boy or girl?
*   Are we ready? Why is this fetus kicking?*

The development of the human brain is a key
*   arena of neurosciences and of the parents.*
Multiplying from a few cells into one of the
*   Most complex nervous system in all nature!*
Is the child learning? Does it have emotions?
*   What occurs during nine months in womb?*

Recently, medical science has discovered clues
of what might be corrected while "invitro!"
Enormously complex maturation occurs during pregnancy so
that careful nutrition occurs.
Careful preparations by parents are essential to nurture the
human being that is emerging.
When poor caring damages health of Mother, the fetus is
impacted by being neglected,
A child's launching into the world may be resilient or spend
a lifetime being handicapped.

"Q's" constructive questions are timed significantly
to influence optimal development.
However, "Q" is overwhelmed with new natural processes,
pregnancy may be problems.
"Alert curiosity" by informed parents can discover
guidelines that provide known "A!"
So that parents, physicians, nurses plus siblings develop
teamwork for this challenge!

Birth and Infancy

Imagine the "Q&A" interchanges when the birthing process
is occurring into the world,
There are numerous features about new infant beyond what
may be known about gender.
Breathing is vital for an infant to inherently do plus a little
assist in normal development.
Obsreticians automatically check so many factors that
parents may not even be curious.

Early impressions are memorable for families with
images that are etched for a lifetime.,
Assessments by professionals help to provide some
guidelines for the "Q" by the parents.
Innumerable "Q&A" exchanges occur within the minds
of parents and naturally siblings,
What other preparations are helpful as we now face
that is beyond our experiences?

Mothers ingeniously anticipate the needs of infants
simultaneously with infant's arrival.
The natural processes of parenting are quickly learned
that are known as developmental.
Of course, "trial and error" is inherent in each birth
experiment that quickly emerges,
Every child becomes a "unique original" as no persons
are ever exactly duplicates.

The intricate combinations of genes are very complex when
just considering an individual.
Identical twins are not completely alike while this may
occur if cloning ever is undertaken.
With hundreds of billion neurons in the brain functions
with many millions of connections,
Nature produces unique individuals who nurtured in a
Wide variety of family environments.

When does an infant develop questions?
This is unknown with even rough estimates.
An infant's brain grows so fast that these minute steps
are only known as approximates.
Recognizing voices, smell, sounds, and faces occur rapidly
in first weeks and months.
Attachments processes are immediately apparent when
a strange face is not "apparent!"

Associating hunger sensations prompts bodily responses
including crying and sobbing.
Nonverbal communications become "basic ingredients
for what are called verbal questions
The quick attention a child receives emotionally,
Physically, significantly and verbally.
These pre-conditioning interactions will soon lead to
verbal questions and exploration.

"Stranger anxiety" is inherent when an infant becomes
upset with unfamiliar care-taking.
Siblings are a key interpreter, comforter and also
problems needing rapt attending.
The bond between infants and caregivers is vital
for the prolonged human development.
Neglected infants survive with unusual capacities
to live but may become handicapped.

Upon mastering elementary language of the family,
infant's growth is then accelerated.
Adults and sibling are bombarded with arrays
of questions as their world is explored.
Parents may become exasperated if they are failing
to appreciate these creative processing.
"Just Because" may become a final response if parents
do not comprehend learning!

Curiosity increases as children investigates themselves
and their own environment.
Their reward in discovering new things to learn helps
to reinforce this type of exploring.
Pupils in Kindergarten and First Grade have an innocent
eagerness to participate.
Creativity rises as their world expands until they encounter
structured learning classes.

The boxes for age and grade plus behavior are vestiges
of the Old Prussian Europeans.
All cultures have schooling for children that are delivered
in a variety of learning models
Learners are impressed with models to Imitate
who are positive and are encouraging.
Stern punishment stifles innate styles of encountering
both their teachers and classmates.

"Learning Environments" are multi-dimensional
with both things to handle and explain.
Effective teaching quickly tunes into the children's unique
interests to then build upon.
Totally structured lesson plans that are pre-packaged
possesses some advantages.
Time schedules in confined classrooms cramp spontaneity
that is a reward in itself.

Recitations are practiced in order to memorize facts
and meanings of curricula.
Pupils are quizzed about answers rather than responding
to their own questions.
They learn quickly that the answers are considered more
important than inquiries.
So many stifle their curiosity in order to comply with the
structured mentalities.

When learners get into the "learning groove," schools can
facilitate what's called "Flow!"
Streams of learning occur like discovering how to master
water currents to destinations.
Cszentmihalyi[27] captures this engrossing process of learning
for its own sake to learn.
Perpetuating inherently the curiosity to discover and
appropriate as part of their team.

---

[27] Czentmihalyi, op.cit.

Questions come naturally to learn how to take the next steps
toward goals of mastery.
"Kids are tuned on!" when these special combinations
Of ingredients come naturally.
Experienced teachers do magical tricks to engage students
with enticements.
These powerful self-rewarding experiences build upon the key.

Building upon innate curiosity of school children is among
the skills of great teachers.
Plus broadening their world with the skills essential
to learn creative problem- solving!
Rote memorization is typical for "taking the next steps"
to attain and reach goals.
Teachers and coaches have similar challenges as practicing
and manipulating tools.

In most cultures, learning to read the key languages
is necessary to master steps.
When reading curricula combine best methods
and individual readiness to grow.
Moreover, pupils learn as much from their smart peers
as much as from teachers.
Reinforcement from family environments as the very
important team members.

Children benefit when they feel comfortable to ask questions
about what their wants.
"Learning environments" include the home, the community
plus, teachers and coaches.
Discovering the dynamics of what "turn a kid uniquely on"
are crucial learning steps,
Both safe structures of school and the open laboratory
of the community do help!

Boys typically collide with the stiff structures of stern schools
more than do girls.
This cramps their adventurous spirit to explore
their environment without controls.
In recent decade, the majority of Hyper Active Disturbance
Diagnoses are males.
This category is often over-diagnosed in order to explain
their school disturbances.

Far too often medications are prescribed to reduce
the hyper activity of boys.
The Medical Profession compounded this pattern as parents
seek to know.
Parents prefer a medical diagnosis rather than a behavioral
problem for relief.
Their own parenting pattern is not accredited to problems but
rather genetics.

These early school years are also when boys have so many
curious questions.
Often challenging authorities like teachers, parents, coaches
and policemen.
When questions are discouraged and punished,
school pupils will conform.
Resulting in stifling of curiosity that is natural
for children wanting to know.

Creativity assessments have dips as structured school grades
that control.
Structured order is demanded that corrals
in physical and mental curiosities.
Memorization is often more and more emphasized
in teaching to pass tests
Stifling ever more and more the explorative inquisitiveness
of these questions.

Empirical Evidence does reveal creativity
and academic achievement.
Increased as a trend while 1980-90
there was a steady creativity decline.
From 1980, creativity assessments of 300,000 school
children were reduced,
Revealing fallacies of using traditional school
achievement tests as measured.

The thrill of discovering something new has its own reward
to reinforce FLOW.

Asking productive questions is essential to nurture
even further exploration.
Traditional schools for the last twenty years
have emphasized memorization,
Not realizing the dated limits of traditionally accepted
answers for questions.

"Top-Down" Deductive thinking is confined
to discovered conclusions.
This method comes from authoritarian propositions
considered important.
In contrast is Inductive method of gathering observations
to be stimulating.
So, processes of discovering regular patterns
become input for questioning.

If answers are more important than questions,
rote learning predominates.
So that questions are discouraged
rather passive acceptance of mandates.

Learners are quick to learn what is rewarded
in contrast to what is punished.
Soon questions are discouraged so answers
become the rewarded response.

A number of Eastern cultures are determined
to pass on historic remedies.
Then rote memorization is rewarded
rather than the pupil's own inquiries.
As processes of original discovering is
given secondary attention therefore.
Instead, school structures reward recitation
of old answers from years before.

Many educators and policy-makers do not recognize
the limits of answers!
Even the answers engineers learned,
are outdated within a year and a half.
If professionals are not taught problem-solving methods
for their challenges.
The half-life of answers is very soon outdated to deal
with current problems.

The school cultures that fail to recognize discovery
and creativity processes.
Short-change students for the key career years
as they address new problems.
Are educational processes now meriting endorsement
by public officials?
Do they have awareness that a number of other cultures
are surging ahead?

The disastrous influence of politicians
and business executive is now acute.
Their previous recommendations that were enacted
were never very astute.
As these officials informed about learning processes
for cultures to succeed?
Are they outdated without assessing the schools
they now try to lead?

There are indications that current decision-makers
are out of current touch?
They are too impressed with answers
without realizing discovery processes.
Unfortunately, they have become impervious to challenges
being protected.
Not up-to-date on but rather how children master
their own education!

D. RESPONDING

Children, Teachers and Scientist are not only questioning!
There are wide spectrums of inquisitive persons wondering!
When Thomas is mentioned as one of the twelve disciples,
Numerous persons call him "Doubting Thomas" surname!

Doubt actually does not comprehend Thomas' contribution,
He asked from integrity what was beyond comprehension.
Thomas honestly asked Jesus to clarify mysterious teachings,
This inquisitive disciple asked in John 14 for help in knowing.

Jesus' reply provides insights about God's many mansions!
Thomas wanted to know, so he provoked Jesus' positions.
"I am the Way, the Truth, and the Life" Jesus did reply,
Thereby informing his followers the Way to be heavenly!

After Jesus crucifixion, Thomas who wanted evidence,
He was shown the facts of Jesus' scars that endured.
The week of isolation in bewilderment prompted a confession,
"My Lord and My God!" now clarifies it for the rest of us!

The probing inquiries by this disciple is reflected in his life,
Thomas took initiative to travel the furtherer way to India!
Is not this impressive evidence of asking questions?
Prompting his responses as factor of Jesus' intentions.

Thomas' Gospel is likewise somewhat mystical,
His insights of relating to Jesus that are very personal!

His spontaneity was derived from intellectual honesty,
Wanting to know so we have faith over doubt as certainty!

Going beyond Thomas' questions to a wrenching tremor,
The contemporary medicine known as "delirious tremens!"
Alcoholics Anonymous continue to be a hope for recovery,
This prompts addicts to realize problems in group therapy.

Alcoholic's physiology becomes medicated with "addictive spirits!"
Their body shudders, quakes and shakes into trembling misery!
When addicts ask for help, most know drying out will be rough!
Asking for help can be admired plus then supported to be tough!

Right Thinking does not just appear quickly "out of the blue!"
This rectifies practices of bad thinking without seeing clues!
While changing to erroneous thinking is a difficult process,
People hold to patterns of cognitive thinking to be depressed!

While "D.T's" are also compounded by additional "D.T's;"
"Disturbed Thinking" has consequences no one might predict,
This is destructive to the person and to their own relationships,
Committed marriages, one partner can damage a partnership!

These disturbances present challenges to family and also to friends,
If someone has "Disturbed Thoughts," others are quickly involved.
Psychological disturbances can benefit from very careful therapy,
It is more readily moved forward if persons raise their uncertainty!

So, when erroneous thinking occurs, questions are significant,
Opening persons concerned by options to search as participants,
Patient persistence is key to respond to these crises entangling,
Cognitive and emotional thinking of those who are searching!

If unexamined certainty lodges in a person's cognitive processes,
When older, they often become more rigid and also impervious.
Crises in functioning and relating will precipitate more searching,
Questions of rigid thinking are key approaches to find real meaning!
Addictive drugs are now an avenue that stressed persons seek,
For temporary relief for the moment, but acute problems later.

Their questions are essential to arrive at a turning point in living,
Without internal searching, outside interventions are very limiting.

Asking constructive questions has not been as significant currently,
Students in schools of the United States are now behind seriously,

Is this unique to now as if these problems happened never before?
Is there precedence if conflicts have occurred known historically?
Examination of regression shows how learning creativity are stifled,
Authoritarian top-down decisions have disastrous future outcomes.
There are examples that show negative evidence of backwardness,
Few are needed illustrating the pattern when authorities regressed.

Disastrous decisions frequently can be turning point in downfalls,
Hitler was a dictator in history whose ideologies were all flawed.
In retrospect, Americans know about outcomes of going to war,
The evidence of the wars in war in Iraq and Afghanistan for sure.
Religious authorities have made decisions that became disasters,
Patterns of trends in papal orders set back scientific discoveries.
Discoveries the earth is the center of this galaxy is an obvious one,
The punishing findings of scientists have set precedence backwards.

When religious authorities fail to be informed about discoveries,
Dominant figures discourage essential growth of most civilizations.
Top-down decisions assume they possess unique universal Truth,
The evidence become a contrary to credibility of authorities is unsafe.
Stance against concepts of evolution are more example as notable,
Uninformed Creationist assumptions believe 6000 years of creation.
Narrow authoritarian position has wide implications for students,
Creating incredibility of authoritarian positions governing futures.

The errors of autocrats in 2011-12 Springs about rebellions,
　　　Reveal obvious as narrow power control makes violent decisions.
Their citizens are victims of these top-down orders from the past,
　　　Will autocrats discover better approaches to include bottoms-up?
Science employs inductive processes to discover of new findings,
　　　Scientists make tentative conclusions, tradition challenges this.
Religious authorities rarely have original discoveries to propose,
　　　Their patterns are to cite top-down deduction from old propositions.

Discovery of new knowledge is vulnerable to top-down suppression,
　　　Because authorities by definition have powers, they often prevail.
There are few air windows that blows fresh breezes thru walls,
　　　Many historical findings are of persecutions and death sentences.

Inertia of old beliefs is amazing resistant to scientific discoveries,
　　　Likewise, cultures resist change contrary to their long-held beliefs.

Cognitive dissonance describes propensity to how on to old patterns,
　　　May deny the truths that are empirically supported by generations.
Why are authorities reluctant to recognize findings of science?
　　　Or original innovations of youth who challenges older persons?
Dynamics of discoveries by younger generations is refreshing,
　　　There is new knowledge that becomes the evidence of futures!

INTERPRETING

Monarchs use theology as justifications for resisting new change.
　　　Rulers may dominate their own knowledgeable persons as strange.
St. Paul was obedient to civil authority he knew as Roman Caesar.
　　　By obeying the civil rulers has fostered more historical exceptions.

There was a key example of Jesus who acceded to Roman "Pilate!"
　　　Did St. Paul not understand dynamics Jesus taught of non-violence?
Obeying rulers presented conflicts of integrity with political ethics,
　　　History recorded tragic conflicts of defying monarchs in conflicts.

Royal crowns and Catholic Popes discovered mutual agreement,
    Church-State relations are troubling with symbiotic arrangements.
Russian Emperors and Orthodox two-headed eagle show alliance.
    Old Monarchs presumed misunderstood Western arrangements.

Arrogance and piety led to history's very dubious combinations,
    Authority figures are duped in original foundations of such sanctions.
Roman Catholic Church and Western States assume justifications,
    For actions as Final Authority designed to protect from being defied.

Authoritarian autocrats govern the religious and civil governments,
    Are notoriously cruel in enforcing violent punishments as mandates.
Imprisonments, exiles and executions as violence used in history,
    Challenge authorities who have fought to perpetuate mean misery.

Heads of civil states ally themselves with wrappings of religious priests,
    Clothing secular authority with religious allegiances to cultural gods.
Political Economy and Theology together become hybrids of mutuality,
    Citizens are subjected to the ruling leadership intended for humanity.!

REFLECTING the SIGNIFICANT LIGHT

The contrast of light is dark!
    Without light this planet is stark!
        Fixed in its orbit without Sunlight
            Our lives would never shine bright!

Light has special significance!
    For People of the Book's existence!
        Including Jews, Christians and Muslims
            Both symbolically and in verbal terms!

The Old Testament has a creation story,
Acknowledges God made light in darkness!
The Scriptures are written to enlighten us
Sacred Rituals also incorporate candlelight!

Jews have candelabra with seven candles
Christians see Jesus as the Light of the World!
Muslim Scriptures enlighten their adherents
"THE BOOK" provides us spiritual guidance!

Stages in Human Development

SEEDING to:
• Nurturing
Cultivating
Communicating
Interacting
Blooming:
Sharing
Serving
Connecting
Teaching
Cross-Fertilizing:

Exchanging
Collegiality
Feedback
Evaluating
Revising
Ripening:

Mentoring.
Expanding Reach
Enlarging Scope
Producing:
Consulting
Writing
Coaching
Harvesting
Reaping
Processing
Storing
Sharing
Going Home
Preparing
Closuring
Departing

INVITATION to TEACH in INDIA, 1998

In 1998, invited to teach in India!
To create a Masters' Degree!
At Union Christian College!
Laying foundation ahead!

Thomas John was my host;
He knew how to get the most.
This was a thrilling new experience,
It included many speaking engagements.

Rotary International gave me a Fellowship!
As I had volunteered my services to help!
Thomas' colleagues were also helpful;
Altogether, this was a real thrill.

Carol joined me the last month!
Women were delighted with her!
Young women aspired to learn
Jointly, we helped them to yearn!

We launched international exchanges!
Over 50 from both of these countries!
Young people expanded experiences;
Adults added their own insights!

These exchanges led to even more!
In 2020, a Doctor of Psychology grew!
The "Endowed Middents Lectureship"
Helped this College with more graduates!

In 2001, a new invitation was extended:
To fill an Endowed UNESCO Peace Chair.

Located at a very large India University;
Manipal University was my destiny!

In 2001, they had a vast enrollment!
Over 50,000 students plus endowment!
They arranged for me to also give lectures;
This was a full range over their nine colleges.

This experience resulted in two books;[28]
These were then very timely works!
Tensions in the Middle East broke,
Resulting in violence abroad!

---

[28] Middents, G., 2001, Crisis in Violence and Peace, Manipal University Press.
Ibid. 2007, BRIDGING FEAR and PEACE: From Bullying to Doing Justice, Manipal
University Press.

After my first lecture, NY City attacked!
Over 3000 Americans were killed!
Catastrophes were extended!
Peace was certainly needed!

Students, faculty and community
Engaged in concerns globally!
The UNESCO Peace Chair
Gave a basis to repair!

My Rotary Hosts were helpful;
Provided platforms to be peaceful!
Global strategies became necessary
Global tensions addressed readily!

This experience was demanding;
It also became very thrilling!
This was the time for peace!
Engaging in big exchanges!

Carol bravely came to India again!
We cultivated some very key linkages!
Again, hosts were thrilled to know her!
Adding credibility for Peace was assured.

Returning home opened many doors;
Rotary, Churches and professionals;

Many invitations were extended;
Building peace and justice further.

Then in 2004, a fourth trip to India,
This time to inoculate children for polio.
Rotary International led this project,
To eradicate polio in all India.

India has tens of millions of children
Now polio is eradicated among Indians.
Plus, it is now also vanished in Africans.
But it is still happening in Afghanistan.

YOGA POETRY

After four trips to India, yoga is natural;
Practiced for 20 years to be familiar.
Yoga is an excellent physical exercise
By engaging one's body to be a prize.

Warming up is also recommended,
Stretching our limbs to be extended.
A floor mat permits laying on one's back
Plus swatting cross-legged or to sit up!

Movements "flow" in a gradual style;
Instructor David always demonstrates.
By showing participants how to engage;
Pacing different stanches whatever age.

Classmates are typically supportive;
Sessions not required but elective,
Participants enjoy yoga after starting;
Then they are glad to be participating.

Yoga is very popular in America!
Need for instructors to teach yoga.
Very little equipment is necessary
Class schedules typically vary.

Participants learn to be silent;
Non-verbal exercise communicates.
Taking part in class is voluntary;
Length of sessions can also vary.

Types of yoga provide options;
"Chair Yoga" for aged sessions!
"Power Yoga" for the muscular;
"Child Yoga" for the youngsters!

Men and women both participate;
Schools find yoga including weights.
Regular schedules have advantages!
Working optimally for adapting bodies.

Unique inclusions of words and phrases;
"OMM..." is rolled out in different stages.
A special vocabulary gains attention;
"Namastae" evokes favorable expression!

"Namastee" is from the Teacher inside me-
To the Teacher inside your—to be happy!
David and other instructors close with it!
Then "Namastee" repeated by participants!

V. PROFOUND PARADOX
Of Human Existence

Orientation

When contemplating the extensive universe in which we all live,
    Provocative thoughts are stimulated for why we are alive.
Astronomers the past two centuries have expanded our worlds,
    As humans are even more insignificant as creation unfurls.

One paradoxical expression may be "Significantly Insignificant!"
    Our existence is so miniscule that we are known as minute.'
In contrast, as creative beings we are "Infinitely so Indefinite!"
    This can also be expressed in the words "Infinitely Finite!"

A paradox describes humans as so "Predictably Unpredictable!"
    We have both consistency, along with being so unreliable.
We have characterized ourselves as being so physically pliable,
    But humans also express terms like "Spiritually Invincible!"

Scientific Investigations

WHAT IS TRUTH?

"The Truth" is a key curiosity of humanity!
    Does anyone comprehend this in societies?
Could "The Truth" be beyond our own bodies?
    Beyond collective brains in this century?

Are humans capable of recognizing limits?
Or should we consider ourselves as "ultimates?"
Are our brains able to reach truthful summits?
Or is this also a peak within human arrogance?

As our universe is explored for dark matter and dark energy,
We simultaneously benefit and overwhelmed scientifically.
When we have conflicting goals can our perceptions be trusted?
How essential are the criteria for science to be objective?

Space explorers now suggest we only know about five percent,
The great unknown is obviously to we humans enormous.
Fortunately, we have come to realize that we are pliably dynamic,
In contrast to earlier beliefs that humans are rigidly static.

We have the capacities to both be so stuck and also stubborn,
We can provoke fellow humans into dynamics of reform.
The processes are considered facet of being transformational,
As a result, we are also involved being repeatedly cyclical.

Spiritual and scientific explorations uncover new developments.
Will we even consider the two forces as being compliments?
The universe "out there" can be explored and be measurable,
Complimenting these objects, prompts what is treasurable.

Our worlds both externally and internally are now expanding,
These forces hopefully help us resist opposite contracting.
We often retreat in the face of fears of the unknown and scary,
Courage is essential for future generations to find bravery.

Foundations of adventure are now being laid into the future,
The spirit of discovery will help human explore nature.
Geologists, archeologists, anthropologists and cosmologists,
Are scientifically investigating the far deepest recesses.

We are also investigating ourselves as inherently in nature,
These are challenges that expect us to be more objective.
Coping with subjectivity may be an impossible expectation,
This forces humans to realize we are part of creation.

Are external observations essential to understand who we are?
Can we accurately examine ourselves while we also care?
This prompts human scientists to confront their limitation,
Objectivity is impossible when we are in transformation.

Unanswered issues require even more profound exploration,
How can the paradox be resolved into accurate formation?
While there have been intriguing discoveries of what is out there,
Are we ready to investigate what is deeply inside us here?

Tentative Observations

The epistemological issues are profound and also disturbing,
How can human creatures still claim to know everything?
If scientists' assumptions hold that only observable is real,
Does this claim presume that humans are vastly surreal?

Less we become inflated with our limited human perceptions,
Perhaps we might consider tempering our exceptionalisms.
Yes, we may be unique on this earth as peak of development,
Does that claim that human beings are nature's ultimate?

Could other unknown intelligence evolving on other planets?
To my knowledge, cosmologists have not more than tenants.
With measures of humility may we earthly humans be cautious,
Might our inflated claims to omniscience be so preposterous?

The mysterious balances of being creatures of a Divine Creator,
Could avail limited human beings of realizing our Originator.

Yes, there are speculations by a few scientists that we are unique,
        Might that claim be feeding our needs to be creation's peak?

Where are the balances of humility within human investigator?
        Are we becoming even more arrogant that claims no Creator?
The awareness of myths of creation long held by human beings,
        Many cultures have encapsulated myths of Divine Creating.

These Transcendental Myths are beyond scientific investigations,
        Science assumes that reality is measurable by <u>homo sapiens</u>.
These conflicts are energy that stimulates further exploration,
        Roots of creativity presume living involves conflicting claims.

Our inquisitive brains stimulate our quest to discover even more,
        Consequently, the natural effects are for us to further explore.
Without creative curiosity we'd be stuck in traditional answers,
        Openly welcoming what could be also alternative responses.

Provocative Intimations

These multiple possibilities provide us hypotheses to investigate,
        Expanding our world of curiosity so that we might not inflate.
These realizations assume that we are open to other explanations.
        Which could balance human beings from renegade
        generations.

Creative conflicts are important even though producing tensions,
        This awareness can contribute to immense further
        extensions.
Learning about the unknown worlds are facets of our experience,
        We can be grateful that there are unexplored more evidence.

Historically these types of creative conflicts are the usual norm,
    What seems unusual is the contrast with tendencies to
    conform.
The pressures to avoid creative tensions are known in reflection,
    Not surprisingly this is the energy about God in His Creation.

These realizations provide a context for what humanity is facing,
    As history unfolds, the participants could find this embracing.
Creation is evolving with small steps that are included overall,
    Our contributions are significant although considered small.

BRAIN INTRICACIES

Yes, more is comprehended than historically!
    No, full comprehensions is still beyond humanity!
Discipline pursuits give awareness and consciousness.
    We are still upon the surfaces of these inquiries!

Our consciousness continues to be a mystery!
    Even among brain researchers scientifically!
Most analyses concern immediate connections!
    Micro- awaiting the macro-brain functions!

Can human beings go beyond our subjectivity?
    Or is objectivity beyond our human inquiries?
New progressive hypotheses are very essential
    For humanity to realize our limited potentials!

Humanity is progressively aware of our boundaries!
    Or are we captive to our own human egocentricity?
Reflection may reveal our limited in comprehension
    Of the complexities that abound in this Creation!

Does empirical evidence show the whole Truth?
Are factual data describing universal worth?
What multi-verses now have different laws?
Will human comprehend that we have flaws?

A. SOCIAL INTELLIGENCE

Civilizations depend on human relations;

Poor and rich whatever their stations.

People thrive when making connections;

Making conversations and raving religions.

Empathy is key in social intelligence;

Complemented by enduring patience.

God displays these essential qualities;

Lubricated by polished sensitivities.

Jesus demonstrated his socializing;

Tuning into people while relating!

His teamwork was highly "contagious;"

God's Grace was his basis to be gracious!

We are called to be faithful human beings;

Loving and ethical in our social connecting.

We benefit from understanding each other;

So that we become sisters and brothers!

ENDING LIFE WITHOUT RIPENING

Most people rarely discuss suicide;

But among groups, it is very wide.

Military veterans have high rates;

Across America in many states!

Suicides need careful consideration;

In my counseling practice 100 cases!

Mostly were depressed young adults

They were dealing with many faults.

Farmers in India are very vulnerable;

With small acreages they feel responsible.

Global warming is a very slow process

From our cars come gas emissions.

In campus ministry, came request from bars;

Help us as Bartenders about our clients.

I had a good conversation in a bar room.

With a Vietnam Veteran who was calm.

He shared a number of his impressions;

After midnight we had a conclusion.

He went on his way while on leave;

This nation unaware what to achieve.

Decades later I was a Vice-Moderator

Of Veterans for Peace planning to meet.

I found a location for a National Convention

It was held 50 years after Japanese Surrender.

These Viet Nam Veterans were very different

From us Korean Veterans and significant.

Many Viet Nam Vets were very troubled;

Drugs and Alcohol widely consumed.

Rehabilitation was badly needed;

Like Veterans of Middle East Wars.

American citizens can provide aid

They fought as our representatives.

Often suicides occur by an impulse;

Not have considered its results.

It may have not been discussed;

With anyone else even related.

Even families may be very surprised;

As a consequence, they may be confused.

Some are likely to experience guilt

"What did we omit and not notice?"

Could suicide ever be seen as ripening?

Many people consider it frightening!

Often seen as a life being unfulfilled

What could persons be if they lived?

Yes, suicide needs immediate attention;

Even global warming should arouse tension.

Suicide happens quickly<>warming slowly;

Intervention is required and done boldly!

During this pandemic, young are worried;

Over 25% have considered suicides! [29]

They felt hopeless while addicted;

Relapses have risen 50 per cent!

Many farmers in India are very suicidal!

If crops fail, they are quite vulnerable.

A new development has occurred

New tractors have really purred!

A recent shift occurs in India,

Farmers now acquired tractors!

Suicides have consequently reduced![30]

Because Farmers' income increased!

---

[29] Kristof, N., Oct. 25, 2020, <u>The New York Times.</u>

[30] <u>The Econnomist,</u> October 17, 2020, "Fertile Ground."

Prices of grain are up this year,

Monsoon rains are also up!

Water reservoirs have filled;

Irrigation has improved!

ACCIDENTS

How will we ever reduce accidents?

High speeding cars in heavy traffic?

Distractions by cell messages;

What are some other reasons?

Vehicles have become weapons!

Drunk drivers are very dangerous!

Or those under the influence of drugs!

Have impaired ways to make judgements.

Heavy traffic takes real patience;

Tired drivers are often sleepy!

Wild kids could be distracting

They can interrupt our driving.

Now big trucks crowd highways;

Their weight makes them weapons!

When crashes have few survivors

These trucks need careful drivers.

All vehicles powered by gasoline,

Add carbon into the atmosphere!

Accumulations become dangerous;

Carbon taxes will hit our purses!

SELECTIVE HEARING and LISTENING

"We hear what we want to hear!"

Humans often do not listen due to fear!

(Of course, our Mothers heard everything)

Gossipers add more than what is said;

To victims, this can become very bad!

To other hearers, it is usually sad!

Many contrary statements are "unheard,"

Worse than hearing that is impaired;

As if pronouncements were unsaid!

Opinions are almost impervious to hear:

As if those disagreeing do not have ears;

Not heard, showing why we need records!

Jesus encountered these human problems;

"Listen to hear" was his own introduction;[31]

So that we give him our full attention!

SOLIPSISM

What is the meaning of this puzzling word?

Does "sol" suggest a term about "The Sun?"

Indirectly, this question makes connections

Suggesting what "rotates around us humans!"

---

[31] Mark 4: 1-24 as Jesus invites to hear his instructive stories.

Solipsism psychologically parallels egocentrism

    Epistemologically, it connotes human subjectivism!

Metaphysically the self includes only the present

    Past and future are excluded as states relevant!

The self knows exclusively its own perception!

    "Self" is considered that center of the universe!

Everything else shall then rotate around me!

    One's own perspective advocates egocentrism!

Do our scientific orientations see "solipsism?"

    As if science is the sole type of verification?

Will "solipsistic" science be aware of limits?

    Or are "The Truths" expressed by Metaphysics?

Metaphysics considers ontology and epistemology!

    "Being" and "How?" do we know full reality?

Our human brain power is just one source!

    Other realms of knowing included in course!

B. AN ATTITUDE of GRATITUDE

By practicing more personal gratitude
We express a more positive attitude!
This provides numerous advances!
Shown by both faith and sciences!

Thankfulness strengthens resistance!
This attitude bolsters immune systems!
It can also lower human blood pressure!
Contributing to our experience of pleasure!

Gratitude also helps better sleeping!
Likewise multiplies by healthier eating!
Then we feel more refreshed awakening!
Plus, benefits greater interest in exercising!

We recover from trauma more quickly!
Gratitude reduces depression & anxiety!

Thereby providing us greater happiness!
We experience less isolation & loneliness!

When we express "Thank You" graciously!
A sensitive receiver smiles appreciatively!
Through practicing "How can I help you?"
Can also enhance our own competence!

Rather than stating refusals as "I can't"
Is conveyed more positively as "I don't."
You can state "No" and not feel guilty,
Provides honest response very readily!

"Let's go!" leads onward to adventure!
With appreciative eagerness for sure!
Practicing "Yoga" can be invigorating!
Along with our personal meditating!

Gratitude helps us to be faithful!
Thankful and faithful as we fulfill!
Expressing thanks to our Creator!
Helps us to even become healthier!

What faith has long already known[32]
Sciences[33] confirm by data shown!
Confirmation displays compatibility
Inspiring us to live more thankfully!

Most of my life was lived in Middle America;

Except for also teaching a year in India.

I was born in Iowa; Live in Minnesota,

Also, military service in New Mexico.

Yes, I traveled south to Venezuela

And also northward up to Alaska!

Briefly, I taught classes in Europe;

Traveled to Rome and also Vienna.

---

[32] Psalm 100, Luke 22: 17-18, Acts 24: 3 in Bible.
[33] Research by University of California, Berkeley scientists! Dallas Morning News, 12/31/2014

A special medical mission to Vietnam

And a conference in European Slovenia.

Also provided consultations in Poland.

Invited to teach at Warsaw University.

But most years lived in Middle America;

On the Great Plains of the United States.

Lived over 600 feet above the sea level.

Visited the East and West Coast briefly,

"PENULTIMATES!"

Might we also recognize our human limits?
    Appreciative of what we know as humans?
Accepting that we are not "The Ultimate?"
    But ready to accept being "Pen-Ultimates?"

This term means "One before the Ultimate!"
    Coming before the final by being resolute!
Knowing we are not the "End" but prior!
    Being ready to recognize what is Earlier!

But not only Earlier but also "Eternal!"
    Beyond time and space in its own realm!
These are not simple inquiries to make!
    Instead raising possibilities to awake!

OLD

PROFESSORS

NEVER DIE!

<>

<>

<>

THEY JUST LOSE

THEIR

FACULTIES!

HOW MANY PROFESSORS

DOES IT TAKE TO CHANGE

A LIGHT BULB?

?

?

?

ONE TO CHANGE IT, AND THREE TO CO-AUTHOR THEIR BOOK!

PROFESSORS?

?

SOMEONE WHO TALKS IN OTHER PEOPLE'S SLEEP!

If all the professor

in the world were

laid end-to-end,

> # They still would not
>
> # reach a conclusion!
>
> **Source: Bulletin: Westminster Theological Seminary,**

C. "THANKSGIVINGS"

Do we serve "the least of these?"
It is Jesus' passionate challenge!
He led all of His own followers!
Providing them with showers!

"The Least" need even more!
They cannot buy it at the store!
They need our caring attention!
As they need more consideration!

Our serving "the slightest of these!"
They need caring that will please!
Jesus provides us with guidance!
Helping the least with assistance!

Thanksgiving is a blessed Holiday!
Deeds are helpful on this festival!
This is an opportunity to now give!
Lifting up anyone who wants to live!

Yes, humanity can become unified;
Even though we are diversified!
Divisions are easily propagated
But humanity can be collected.

Unity [34]is a blessing from God;
Bringing together all separated.
This is the glue for our cohesion;
God gives the gift of unification!

We so easily have devious divisions,
Politically, athletically, economically.
Humans can be dividers or unifiers
Can we now become peacemakers?

Worshiping God brings us together!
Praying jointly to our Heavenly Father.
Looking to God who is our Healer;
Jesus is known as "The Deliverer!"

Our world of nations needs "community!"[35]
This mission is our clear opportunity!
Yes, bringing together is our duty!
With physical and spiritual energy!

HAPPINESS<>JOY[36]

Although related, but not the same;
Both help people deal with pain.
How are they different or similar?
Let us explore what is so familiar.

---

[34] Psalm 133.

[35] The New Testament, Romans 6: 5, Colossians 2: 2 and 2: 14.

[36] Biblical sources: Philippians 2: 2; James 1: 2; I John 1: 4; II John 1: 12; III John 1: 4.

Happiness comes from external experiences;
It usually occurs as we bubble with cheer.
Joy stems from deeper within a person;
Moreover, joy is usually more permanent!

We can cultivate joy in several ways:[37]
1-Meditating as we live in the present.
2-We can embrace the extraordinary;
3-We can help others very personally.

Happy times with others around us;
Engaging intentionally for experiences.
Good fellowship, and also good food!
These are occasions when we feel good!

May Thanksgiving and Christmas be full of joy;
May your happiness also happen on holidays!
Carol and Jerry extend our very best wishes;
So let some else now do kitchen dishes!

"BEYONDERING!"

This term may now be briefly comprehended:
"Beyond what we humans have predicted!"
Beyonders go further than ever expected!
From early forecasts that were outed!

Expressed in hypotheses of multi-verses!"
We have evidence of billions of galaxies!
Each with millions of suns and planets!
What might be other expanses of realities?

---

[37] Schneider, Jamie, Assistant Editor at <u>mindbodygreen.</u>

Solipsism is insufficient to appreciate
Many solar systems would be expansive!
Beyond narrow self-centered perspectives
So that this solar system is one elective!

"The Music of the Spheres" is boundless!
Beyond the realms of just one universe!
Creation by Divine Power is inclusive!
Countering narrow scope to be exclusive!

Augustine[38] recognized "Our Souls are Restless!"
"Until we eventually find our rest in Thee!"
He possessed awareness of Greek Philosophy
Was influenced by Aristotle's methodology!

BEYOND CREATION of this UNIVERSE

Yes, the human brain is an amazing organ!
Possibly the greatest of living organisms!
Does it qualify for knowing ultimate reality?
Is this question to be decided by humanity?

Advanced science now encounters uncertainties!
Creation if filled with numerous complexities!
Currently science recognized many mysteries!
Waiting to be investigated with methodologies!

How extensive will the universe ever expand?
So far, human awareness does not understand!
Is space endless without limited boundaries?
Mathematics already has the concept of infinity!

---

[38] Augustine, The City of God, 4th Century A.D.

In time, will human brains grow to understand?
        Who can now investigate to discover an answer?
Scientific technological methods are challenged
        How to design verification with research studies?

Are there issues that confront our limitations?
        Now time, this question provides consternation!
Now human knowledge is certainly amazing!
        How extensive will it continue growing?

Now this is the time for our hair-greying!
        It is a clear indication of our ripening!
Our collective wisdom is accumulating!
        Be ready now for poetry publishing.

D. GLOBAL ANTHEM II

Citizens of <u>Gaia</u>, our Mother Earth,
We have known you since our birth!
As teammates on this Created Earth,
We give you gratitude for our worth!

As we live in this time and this space,
Teammates know this is our place.
Our words give Mother Earth honor,
To YOU our respect we now offer!

Gravity holds planets here together
As athletes, we thank our Creator.
Orientals & Occidentals on earth!
Spanning from South also North!

Respecting opponents & teammates,
We grow mutually as true athletes.
We live in justice and in harmony,
Peaceful is just how we want to be.

We're not here on Gaia accidentally,
Believe in God's own intentionality!
As athletes we are willing to sacrifice,
We know that He paid for our price!

In discipline, you are our neighbors,
Loving You, we hope as You do us.
Jointly we ca<u>n he</u>lp Gaia peacefully,
Ethically doing Justice sustainable.

Bibliography

Augustine, The City of God, 4th Century A.D.

Barnett, C., 2015, Rain: A Natural and Cultural History, Crown Press.

Johnson, 1967 Yale University Dean in a personal communication while both served on a committee for assessing standards exams for ordination in the UPC USA.

Louis, Henry, April 18k, 2011, "Skip Gates, Jr., and Holds Everyone Accountable," Newsweek. And Lisa Miller, pp. 42-45, "Skip Gates Next Big Idea."

Koskela, D (2015) Calling and Clarity: Discovering What God Wants for Your Life, Eerdmanns.

Middents, G., 1973, "The Relationship of Creativity and Anxiety," The Journal of Religion and Health.

Ibid., 1976, "Procedures for Assessing Pre-Medical Students," The Journal of Medical Education

Ibid, 2001, Crisis in Violence and Peace, Manipal University Press.

Ibid. 2007, BRIDGING FEAR and PEACE: From Bullying to Doing Justice,

, G., 2018, Personal Meaning DeMystified, iUniverse Publications, Bloomington, Indiana.

Ibid, Connecting Sports and Religions, iUniverse Publications, Bloomington, Ind.

Ibid., 2020, Earthlings & Spacelings! Legaia Books.

I Timothy 6:7 in the New Testament of the Bible

Middents, G., 1976, "Procedures for Assessing Pre-Medical Students," The Journal of Medical Education

Ibid., 1973, "The Relationship of Creativity and Anxiety," The Journal of Religion and Health.

Middents, G., 1973, "The Relationship of Creativity and Anxiety," The Journal of Religion and Health.

Nagel, Thomas, 2012, Mind and Cosmos: Why the Materialist Neo-Darwinism Conception of Nature is Almost

Certainly False, Oxford University Press.

Ibid., verses 6:8 "But if we have food and clothing we will be content with these!"

Piff, Paul, el.al., 2012 "Higher Social Class Predicts Increased Unethical Behavior,"

Schneider, Jamie, Assistant Editor at mindbodygreen.

The Econnomist, October 17, 2020, "Fertile Ground."

Books Published by AUTHOR:

Personal Meaning DeMYSTIFIED, 2018, iUniverse Press.
CONNECTING ASIANS and AMERICANS, 2019, LEGIA BOOKS.
CREATIVE BEYONDERING, 2019, McNAUGHTON Press.
EARTHLINGS and SPACELINGS, 2020. Legaia Books.
SPORTS and RELIGIONS TOGETHER, 2020, iUniverse Press.
HEATING the EARTH: GLOBAL WARMING, 2020, iUniverse Press.
PSYCHE HISTORIES: PRESIDENCIES and FIRST LADIES., 2020, iUniverse Press.

Author's Background:

Gerald "Jerry" Middents' has had wide experiences after serving as a US Air Force Captain. He became a Presbyterian Minister and earned a Ph.D. He served on the faculty of Austin College and is now Professor Emeritus of Psychology.

Invitations came to teach at Universities in India, China, Poland and Slovenia. He taught at Mahatma Gandhi University primarily at Union Christian College. Then he was invited to fill the Endowed UNESCO Peace Chair at Manipal University in India. Lecture invitations came from University of Texas at Dallas, Ljubljana U., Mangalore U., St. Paul's College, five medical schools, six seminaries and several community colleges.

He has been a member of Rotary International since 1946. He has addressed dozens of Rotary Clubs in the United States and India. Twice he was supported by Rotary University Teaching Grants. He has been awarded "Four Avenues of Service Above Self."

He provided programs at the World Congress of Organizational Development Institute in Nepal, Slovenia, Wisconsin and Mexico plus taught courses in Stockholm and Switzerland.

His poetry books includes _Personal Meaning DeMystified_ plus _Heating the Earth: GLOBAL WARMING, EARTHLINGS and SPACELINGS,_ after publishing other books, journal articles, sermons and lectures. Creativity is his special interest in global policy for peace and justice.

Printed in the United States
by Baker & Taylor Publisher Services